Fundamental Magick

Casey "Jones" Erdmann

Fundamental Magick

ISBN: 979-8-9863555-0-4
WEBSITE: https://echosbox.com/

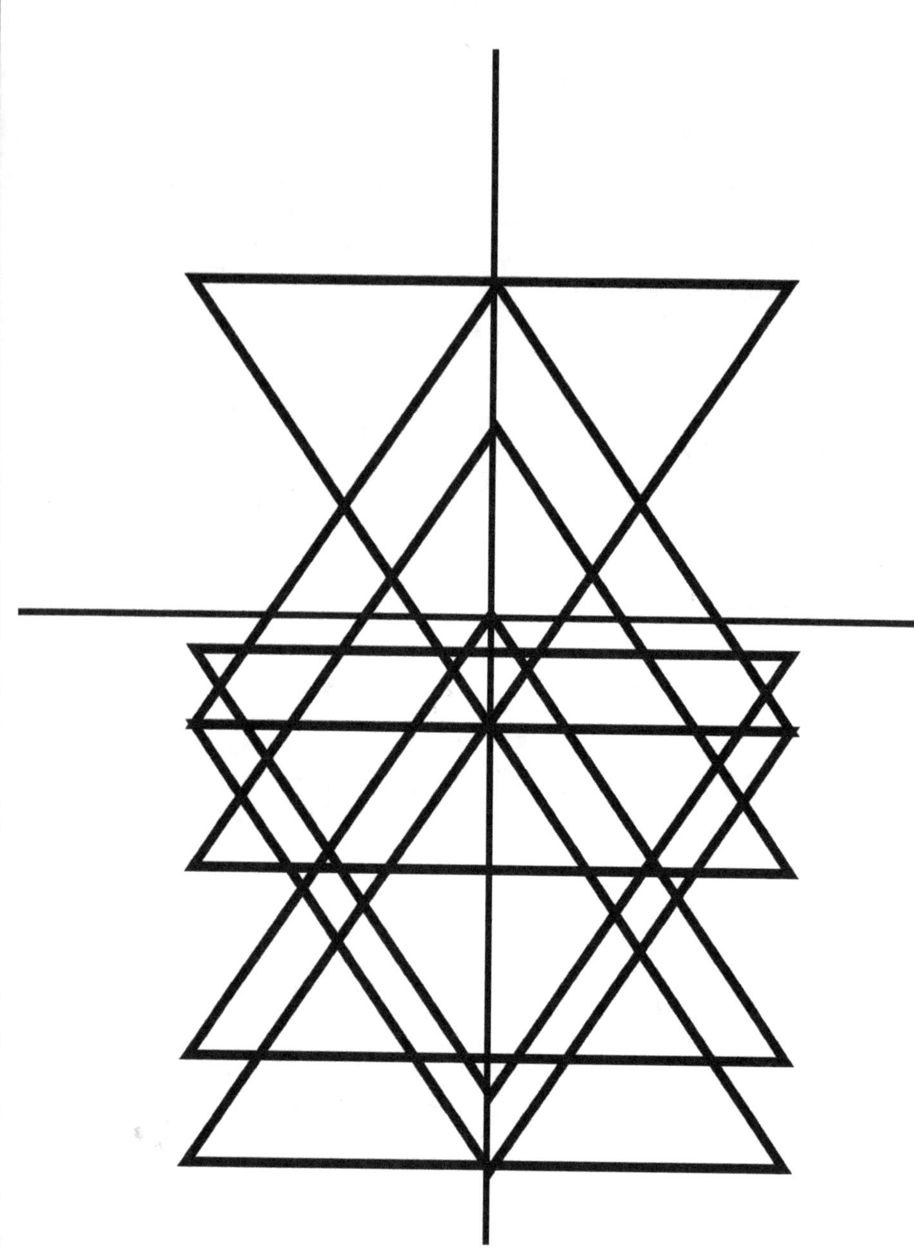

Hexagram Collage - Represents the 4 Hexagrams in the LBRH and LIRH sealed by the Qabalistic Cross

Table of Contents

This text is dedicated to all the teachers I have learned these practices from, as well as the students learning from the path being set forward from here on.

A special thank you of love, gratitude, and respect to:

✦ Damien Echols
✦ Jason Louv
✦ Duncan Trussell

You all have inspired my growth from afar for many years. I wouldn't know all that I do without you and I am forever grateful for the positive change brought to my life by your work. I intend for my work to continue this change in others.

Prologue

Life, in terms of what existence means to the individual, is not accessible to all, but is somehow the default. We are somewhat required to "live" until we achieve enough maturity and consciousness to determine what life even is. All over the world the life that is experienced comes with a vast array of complexity. Some of this complexity makes it simply hard to survive, much less thrive. Even more confusing are the barriers that become created artificially over time. Despite the nature of any barrier that exists in life, they are all very real, artificially created or not. Fortunately, just as there are infinite complexities as they relate to difficulties in life, there are also infinite complexities for peace and love.

This text serves as a supporting reference to teach the most effective and life changing fundamentals to allow the whole of humanity to not just survive, but thrive. The path this text will open for many is not one that is accepted by all, but it is one that is open to all. It is also not the only path in life. Many traditions and practices, both secular and spiritual, exist that can very much achieve the same goal of Ceremonial Magick. If you gather nothing else from this text, understand that your life is yours, and the assertion of this text is that you should be wholly yourself no matter the path you take. Do what benefits you, but bring good to all as you do so.

"Always try to be nice, but never fail to be kind" - Steven Moffat/Peter Capaldi

Unicursal Hexagram - Symbol of Thelema

Chapter 1: Ceremonial Magick

"First of all, you're already doing magick. With every thought, word, and deed you are influencing the world around you and determining what comes your way..." - Damien Echols - High Magick , Page 3

Those of you who are choosing to read this book are likely at least familiar with what "magick" is, but for those that may be diving in out of sheer curiosity, this chapter will introduce it in as approachable of a manner as possible. Magick is not a religion, or some strange set of cult practices. Magick at its core is simply another option for a spiritual path in life. Ceremonial Magick in particular is a set of practices that pulls from traditions as early as the Abrahamic religions (such as Judaism, Islam, and Christianity) all the way through Norse Paganism, Buddhism, and even ancient Babylonian practices. Think of Ceremonial Magick as a sort of meditation practice, with similar goals of self improvement and enlightenment, but at an extremely accelerated rate. Often a good parallel to compare the end goal of Ceremonial Magick to is that of most eastern meditation traditions. Many of these systems aim to achieve the exact same thing Ceremonial Magick does, and are quite effective at it. The difference is that many of these systems often aim to achieve this state of consciousness and self awareness throughout multiple life times. Ceremonial Magick aims to achieve it in one.

Common Questions

Based on that introduction you may have a few common questions. I know I did when I first started so let's call those out. If magick isn't a religion or a set of cult practices, why is it often coupled with the idea of "the occult"?

✦ Magick of any sort stands on its own as a practice. Simply put, it is accessible, malleable, and timeless. This means it can be integrated into any religion, cult, order, or group. In fact as this text addresses later, to this day modern Christian traditions, all the way to traditions incorporated into modern Satanism, both have rituals that are direct practices of Ceremonial Magick. Because of this many "occult" practices choose to integrate some practice of magick into their traditions as well because they can, and it works. In fact that is what *the occult* means. It's not something necessarily "evil" or "dark", it's simply defined as "matters regarded as involving the action or influence of supernatural or supernormal powers or some secret knowledge of them" (8). Most mystical and spiritual practices integrate some sort of magick, even if they don't call it that. As stated above, even modern religions do so.

As stated in the quote from Damien Echols prefacing this chapter, you are already doing magick right now.

So far Magick as a concept has been asserted and "Ceremonial Magick" has been mentioned, but are there other types of Magick too?

✦ Absolutely, while this text is primarily focused on Ceremonial Magick, there are many established and structured forms of Magick. There are even synonymous names for various practices. For example, Ceremonial Magick is also known as "High Magick". Other practices include "Natural" or "Low" Magick, Chaos Magick, Folk Magick, etc... This list can go on and on. While this text does focus on Ceremonial Magick, what is beautiful about doing so is that it is a foundational practice that incorporates all practices (or that other practices derive influence from). In fact, while the practice of Ceremonial Magick is the focus of this text, it will also cover various very relevant practices of what could be considered as Natural Magick. These strengthen a Ceremonial Magick practice even further. Especially for beginners learning fundamentals.

Why is it being spelled with as "magick" instead of "magic"?

✦ This question is always the most basic and semantic, and as a result, fortunately has the most basic and semantic answer. It is simply to distinguish "stage magic" from a practice of "spiritual magic" when writing. Stage magic would be magic that you see performed as a show for entertainment. Usually this is based on techniques such as sleight of hand, illusion, and feats of abnormal physical accomplishment (like holding your breath under water for an extremely long time). Stage magic, or prestidigitation, is entertainment. It is not spiritual in any way on its own. So in order to distinguish the two, as stage magic rose in popularity, practitioners of "spiritual magic" appended the "*k*" just to make things obvious. Ultimately the spelling doesn't matter as long as the word is prefaced with the correct connotations surrounding the communication medium of choice. For consistency's sake, most magickians append the "*k*" just to be extra clear. To the uninitiated this is also a nice visual indicator that something is off, so if you had this question to start with then congratulations, that was part of the point!

Basic Psychology

Before diving further into Ceremonial Magick there are a few topics worth covering to ground one's understanding. It would be overwhelming to throw one into a meditation practice or a ritual blindly. That said, if you would like to skip ahead you are welcome to, but that is not recommended. Now that we've defined Ceremonial Magick at a high level it is important to break down the base components of it. While it is a spiritual practice at the end of the day, it is one with very practical, and at times, physical roots.

If you remove the spiritual component from Ceremonial Magick you are actually left with a basic set of psychological exercises that aim toward general self improvement. In fact if you have ever been to therapy and received some sort of exercise or handout, these types of handout exercises accomplish the same goal in the respect of psychological self improvement. Let's use a common exercise of self validation for example. A therapist or psychologist may ask you to think critically of yourself in a positive way. One common exercise might be to sit down and acknowledge what you have accomplished today, validate that accomplishment, and recognize it no matter how small. This can help some people to grow into a mindset of recognizing even more accomplishments, big or small, and validate their achievements within them to improve one's over all mental health. In Ceremonial Magick one might do the exact same thing, but instead use meditation and imagery, like sigils, to focus their mind on the achievement. One may even use it as a practice to make progress on an achievement that has not yet occurred.

This is the bare minimum benefit of Ceremonial Magick. Some people are content with this benefit and never move along to the further purposes of this practice. There's nothing wrong with that choice, but it's important to acknowledge that while Ceremonial Magick does provide an outlet for self improvement, that is not the end goal. Stopping after basic self improvement by choice leaves a lot on the table, but everyone's journey is unique. As previously stated, magick of any sort is not the only option for a path of growth in life.

Up to this point we've acknowledged the idea of "spirituality" pretty heavily. Does this mean you have to believe in a "God" or "Gods" to practice magick? Absolutely not, but it will require you to broaden your understanding of how the universe works and be accepting of more abstract ideas. This text will document a lot of practices that reference Abrahamic religions. This is because Ceremonial Magick is a western tradition at heart, and the rituals and structures created for this work have correspondences that have been heavily researched over the years. You are free to modify these any which way you want, but in order to do so you have to understand the formulas by which they were constructed. For example, if you consider yourself an atheist, you may not wish to issue a prayer to a God you don't believe in. You would be free to change a ritual to suit the more practical and psychological aspects surrounding it. In doing so however, you must be sure you understand the formula for whatever it is you're modifying in order to gain the same benefit. This might be one of the most interesting things about Ceremonial Magick. In fact this practice is what can be referred to as a "spiritual science". As Arthur C. Clarke once famously said, "Magic's just science we don't understand yet". In fact as time passes, some of the ancient practices founded by Ceremonial Magick could become dated and less effective than a modern replacement. It doesn't mean they will stop working, but as life goes on we may come up with better alternatives to achieve the same goal. For example, if a new chemical was discovered that could permanently enlighten someone and could be distributed as medicine...well why wouldn't we use that instead? That is just as "magickal" as any ritual. It's all about what works.

Spiritual Science

Why refer to Ceremonial Magick as a "spiritual science"? All the rituals and practices in this text are hypothesis that are derived from carefully calculated correspondences based on how the universe works at a practical level. Of course, we don't know fully how the universe works, so Ceremonial Magick sort of reverse engineers these hypothesis by examining how the world around us operates and impacts us day to day. By emulating that in our own lives, this practice aims to reflect the workings of the universe and cause practical change in our little microcosm of a life. In simpler terms that means you can try anything in this book and treat it like an experiment. Some people experience incredible change from all these practices, some experience nothing at all from some, but find that one particular practice really works for them. What's also interesting is that even if nothing seems to work for you, you can take the formulas that you learn and create a practice for yourself that does. Keep in mind, it cannot be emphasized enough that it is a *spiritual* science, so if you stunt yourself by removing that spiritual component you'll only grow in one direction. Simply be aware of that, but ultimately everyone's path and practice is unique to them, so if that's your goal, then that is excellent! Knowing what

you want out of these practices is a huge part of getting
exactly that. You will only receive that which you put in.

Control

Once you begin these practices it is important to know
that you are in control of your life now. You may think you
already are, but the reality is, no one is. How do we know
this? Well if we were in total control of everything we
experience in life we could easily do whatever we want. For
example, I can't just make everyone around me fall in love
with me, and neither can you. Keep in mind everyone has
their own influence and will, and it isn't really possible to
truly control others, perhaps you can influence someone
heavily, but not puppeteer their true will. However, it is
absolutely possible to fully control yourself. Back to basic
psychology again, you may not be able to control other
people's emotions, but you can control yours and how you
respond. It is exactly the same concept with Ceremonial
Magick. You can't control the world with Ceremonial
Magick, that is not the point, but you can control your life
and how you respond to the world around you. This allows
you to influence your life, the universe, and ultimately live
the life you want to live as the person you want to live it as.
It is a medium for infinite change and infinite possibilities.

Why is this important to be aware of though? Well often
in life we may find it easier to blame our unhappiness or
lack of well being on external factors. Once you become a

magickian this is no longer an option. That doesn't mean external factors aren't the source or cause of any discomfort, that is a natural part of life. What it does mean is you control how you respond to and influence those factors. If you choose to wallow in what is thrown at you, you ignore your power to do something about it. When you practice Ceremonial Magick there is no longer room or space to blame others. You are in control, if you want change, it's up to you to cause it.

Ceremonial Magick gives you the power, knowledge, and practices to focus you heart, mind, body, and soul on exactly what it is you want to achieve. By starting these practices you are no longer living life on "autopilot" but taking direct control of the steering wheel. This can sound terrifying, but once you have done it then you can accomplish quite literally anything you put your mind to. It can also be a lonely path. By nature your practice is yours, no one can tell you what is right and wrong, only what is traditional, effective, and recommended. As a result communities for Ceremonial Magick are very small outside official orders that are dedicated to it. Books like this, along with authors and teachers like Damien Echols and Jason Louv, aim to finally close that gap with their work. This progress is world altering, but it will take more time. Ultimately the nature of Ceremonial Magick is lonely, but that does not mean we can't find community within it. It simply means in practice, it's up to you. No one is going to make you do, say, or change anything. You have to keep it up on your own. Even if you have a teacher, they will not hold your hand. Books are often equivalent to a teacher in the respect that you use them to take in information and practice. Often teachers are simply teaching from a book. If not it is from experience they have acquired over time that could also be documented in a book, video, podcast, presentation, etc...

That is not to say having a teacher isn't valuable, it absolutely is, and some used to say it was necessary in Ceremonial Magick. It was how the "current" of magick was traditionally passed. Fortunately it is not at all required and more and more people are able to self-initiate simply by starting the work. The concept of the "current" comes from this idea that Magick of all kinds traditionally was handed down from person to person verbally. It was a spoken tradition, similar to how many religions and stories from history were only carried on by those that told them. This was how information flowed up until times where humanity began documenting things in writing. Magick has finally reached a point where it is no longer necessary to teach by spoken word traditions alone. This, in addition to removing the veil of secrecy kept by classic orders you may learn about in your studies, has made magick in all forms far more accessible than it used to be.

The Great Work and True Will

After alluding to different concepts such as "paths" and "practices" you may be wondering what the actual point of Ceremonial Magick is. Traditionally speaking, Ceremonial Magick aims to help you achieve the concept of what is known as "The Great Work" (TGW). This concept has changed over the years, but in modernity it is the same thing as achieving enlightenment, completing the "solar body", or "becoming one with the universe" as described by other traditions with the same goal. Practically speaking, it really is whatever you want it to be based on your own personal beliefs. That said, if you don't emphasize spirituality it is no more than a psychological avenue for self help. This is why concepts like TGW have been the core goal of Ceremonial Magick since its birth, same with any other similar practice. This asserts that there is simply more to life than what we experience in our lifetime through our lens of life as people. Achieving TGW essentially means that once you die, your consciousness disperses out into the universe and becomes one with "the source". What is "the source"? Well some call that "God", some call it "The Big Bang", you could even call it something ridiculous like "A Ball of Yarn". The point is it is nameless and we only understand what it is based on what science observes and what history teaches. A universal truth is that the universe is moved by energy, everything that interacts with anything is exerting some sort of energy. Ceremonial Magick asserts that there is a source of all this energy, and this source is responsible for all of creation in the universe. Further it asserts that this source is simply everything. It is you, it is me, it is the page of this text you are flipping through. The whole purpose is for the energy to infinitely experience itself. So call it whatever you like, but your goal is to connect with this assumed source of energy and ultimately return to it consciously. If this sounds a little out there, don't worry, skepticism is healthy. That's exactly why covering the idea of a "spiritual science" is important. Be skeptical, try it out for yourself. What you'll find is that it either works, or it doesn't and you are free to draw your own conclusions from there. This book wouldn't exist if there wasn't some truth in it all, but never take someone else's word for it when it comes to spirituality, experience it for yourself.

What happens practically when you achieve TGW? Well on a physical level you will have achieved your "true will". The concept of a "true will" is a bit abstract and unique depending on the individual. The easiest understanding is that you will experience what you are supposed to truly experience in this lifetime and throughout eternity from the perspective "the source". When you complete TGW and become "one with the universe" (or however you prefer to phrase it) you will be experiencing your entire consciousness and exerting what you are meant to exert through the lens of "the source". This is because at that point, essentially you are the source. What's interesting is that is true even now. We are all derived from the same space junk and energy that created it all. We are all *already* one with "the source", we simply aren't experiencing it as such by default. Instead "the source" is experiencing life through us. Magick lets us flip that in reverse. The concept of changing our consciousness to begin to experience our true will is known as many things, but in Ceremonial Magick it's often referred to as "crossing the abyss" or "piercing the veil". These terms come from a lot of the energetic visualizations magickians have experienced when achieving TGW, and is a simple way to describe them from a visual perspective. Don't get too hung up on that for now, it will begin to make more sense as you dive into this work, but do be aware of this concept as starting a practice without being aware of the purpose can be just as confusing, if not worse.

Holy Guardian Angel

The final introductory concept to understand before diving into the material is the "Holy Guardian Angel" (HGA). In Ceremonial Magick your work will guide you to "achieve the knowledge and conversation of your HGA". Remember that phrase, as memorizing it will prepare you for some of the practices ahead. This is your first goal as a Ceremonial Magickian and it may take you quite some time. Basically the concept of the HGA is the same thing as becoming self aware and "awake", so even if you don't believe in the Abrahamic deities and angels that will be referenced that's totally fine. You can and will still experience this shift in consciousness. The idea of an angel is just a tool used to abstract and experience the shift in a more powerful way. It is strongly advised to stick to working with these entities as a beginner no matter what you want to call them. Regardless if you choose to consider them to be abstract psychological concepts, or actual angels, they are very real and very powerful. The HGA is the first step in "crossing the abyss". Once you do that, while books of this nature will continue to be valuable resources for you, they will no longer be necessary to continue TGW. You will begin to experience life as a whole, complete person, and act on your true will to eventually complete TGW and achieve "enlightenment".

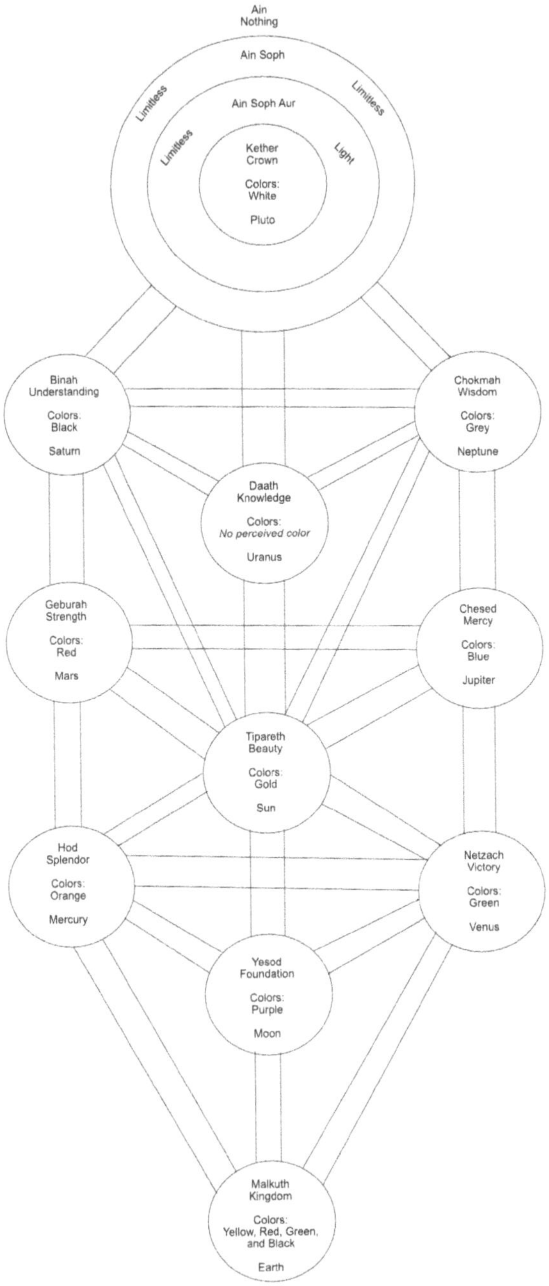

Tree of Life - Qabalistic Technical Diagram

Chapter 2: Visualization

Visualization is an extremely important part of any magickal practice. Especially if the practice involves any sort of meditation work. It becomes even more critical when introducing the complex rituals that require it. As you'll learn, Ceremonial Magick uses visualization heavily, but what is it?

In the context of meditation and Ceremonial Magick alike, visualization is kind of like seeing a memory in your mind and replaying it. In meditation that's almost exactly what it is, the only difference being that you are creating a new memory in a way. Later on when you learn different meditation techniques you may be asked to visualize a bright white light, or to feel and see yourself sitting against a tree. This can come easy to some, and be more difficult to others, but it's important to master before moving onto ritual work. This is because ritual work requires you to visualize with your eyes open at times, meaning you are seeing and projecting what you visualize into reality before you. This might kind of sound like forcing yourself to hallucinate, and depending on how focused and intense you create your visualizations, it absolutely can be just that. That said, it's absolutely not necessary for visualizations to be intense.

Some advice from Jason Louv is to just make sure you are focused and committed to whatever visualization you can come up with. For example, if you can't feel a tree in a physical manner while meditating, or maybe the light isn't quite as bright as you'd like to see it, then that's okay. Just keep your focus on the exercise and the end goal. It doesn't matter that your white light wasn't booming and glowing in your mind. As long as you focused on it and completed the exercise you will see the same result. This is critical to know and understand because everyone's brain works differently. Some people can't see a powerful angel or brilliant flaming pentagram vividly before them, if at all, but you can make your brain represent it somehow and direct your focus towards that. Over time you'll get better and better at visualizing different things, it comes by nature of the practice. Even if you never get things to exactly match a traditional exercise, you'll have your own version of it, and as long as you reap the same benefits, the rest is just a tool to help you get there.

In fact, as I have learned from Damien Echols, a skilled magickian can exert great energy with a flick of a ring on their finger. No visualization, no tools, no imagery necessary, just complete control. You won't have that at first, but you shouldn't, and you also may not prefer to act on your will that way even if you can. Sometimes it's just easier to use the tools that are established, that's the whole point of them. Do realize though, that there may be times where you have nothing but yourself. You could be in a situation such as a vacation away from your normal wares, or even as extreme as being dropped on an island with nothing but the clothes on your back. With this in mind, even if you choose to practice with tools, be sure you can always do the same techniques with nothing at all, even if it requires modification. This is where visualization strength, and understanding the formulas of these practices becomes the most important thing. You should always be able to do magick no matter where you are or what you have.

This book will teach the use of the "empty hand" technique. This means you need nothing do to these practices except yourself, and knowledge of the practice. Different tools will be addressed as they pertain to a given exercise so you are free to adapt and use them as you wish, but they will not be expressly required or taught in any depth on purpose. This is because they truly aren't needed to do magick, even if they are useful and beneficial. This will give you a strong foundation in Ceremonial Magick that you can use anytime, anywhere.

To begin familiarizing yourself with visualization try the basic practice detailed in this chapter. The goal is simply to feel control over what you see in your mind and essentially imagine anything, even without meditation. In fact that is exactly what you are doing, imagining something. The object of a burning candle is recommended for this exercise, but feel free to visualize anything you'd like to think of in the present moment.

Visualization Exercise

Start off by finding a quiet place. Feel free to sit, stand, or even lay down. Just be sure you are comfortable and able to focus. Once you have created a space to think and focus, begin taking deep breaths. Don't worry about how many, or how shallow, or how deep. Just breathe and focus on your breathing for a bit. Once you only notice your breathing, take that focus and begin following these steps:

1. Close your eyes and think about a white candle stick. Visualize it unlit and just sitting there. You can try to see it sitting on a candle holder or a table, but as long as you just see it to the best of your ability that is more than enough.
2. Continue breathing but focus on the unlit candle. Sit with this image for as long as you can. Try counting to 60 if you can before moving on. If you can hold the visualization for longer than that feel free to do so, and move on when you feel ready.
3. Now light the candle. To do this simply begin to visualize that the candle is now lit. If you need something practical, see yourself light a match or ignite a lighter to it. This may be more difficult than simply imagining it being lit suddenly, but try whatever works for you until it is lit.
4. Watch the candle burn. Try to hold the visualization until the candle burns out. In order to do this you must see the lit candle burning and melting as a real candle would in front of you.

5. Try speeding up or slowing down how fast the candle is melting. If you can't that's okay, this is just a sample exercise in controlling the visualization. Simply holding the image of the lit candle for as long as you can is enough.

6. Once you feel you have done all you can, clap your hands or snap your fingers to reset your focus, and open your eyes. This is just a physical cue to capture your focus back to reality. Simply opening your eyes will work as long as you are able to easily reestablish your focus on your own.

Feel free to repeat this exercise over and over again until you feel confident enough with your visualization technique to move on. Even if you're unsure, you may simply try moving on and see if the exercises in the next section feel achievable to you. If not, return here and repeat this exercise. All of the exercises will require large amounts of repetition to truly master, but you will know you are ready to progress once it becomes natural and familiar to you. If this is brand new to you try practicing it two or three times a day, at least until it becomes comfortable. Don't rush, it is important to take all the time you need. Remember you are doing this for yourself, you will achieve what you need to achieve when you are ready to achieve it. Just keep doing the work.

Third Eye - Depiction of the third eye representing an awakening of the conscious and subconscious

Chapter 3: Basic Energy Work

Before diving into the various meditations that will benefit your practice, it's actually time to do our first bit of magick. As stated in the first chapter, the entirety of the universe operates on one universal truth that we are all aware of. That truth is, the universe runs on a constant, infinite, flow of energy. This can be observed by analyzing the first law of thermodynamics. That is "energy can be neither created nor destroyed, but only changed from one form to another" (4). This law further states as an example that "if heat is recognized as a form of energy, then the total energy of a system plus its surroundings is conserved." (4). That second part is very interesting as whatever medium of energy you choose as the example, the second part is still true. This means that the total energy of the universe is a constant. It is ever present.

If you take this further, the second law of thermodynamics states that "energy must be conserved in any process involving the exchange of heat and work between a system and its surroundings" (5). This works in tandem with the first law simply meaning that any energy that is exchanged is fully conserved in the process and cannot be transferred in such a way that creates more energy. It can only be transformed in an equal way that conserves all energy. Now you may be wondering, where does magick fit into all of this?

Well if you dig a little deeper there is a theoretical concept known as the "perpetual motion machine". This machine is able to create and run on its own energy, meaning it can run forever. Currently creation of this machine is impossible, however it is possible to create a machine that can extract limitless amounts of energy from its surroundings (let's say the basic four elements of earth, air, fire, and water) and turn that into something else in an infinite process. While the second variation of the machine is possible, it's only possible because it does not violate the first law of thermodynamics as energy is still conserved and transferred into new work. Still, neither of these machines exists, or do they?

That's where magick comes in. The universe itself *is* the current perpetual motion machine based on the the present definition of this theoretical idea. If we acknowledge the universe to be an infinite representation of energy being put to work, which is arguably observable with every breath you take, then this means we exist within this machine. Magick works by allowing us to essentially become the second version of that machine. The goal of many practices in magick is to take the energy already provided by the universe around us and convert it into something else that meets our goals. You can use your own internal energy, but that is only because your body naturally creates and uses energy from the universe in its day to day functions. If you use your own energy in a practice then you will quickly drain yourself and have to constantly restore yourself. This is why we eat and sleep, to rest and restore our natural energy.

Magick teaches you to cut out the middle work that is your own energy, and directly use the energy of the universe around you so you don't have to rest all the time just to participate in these practices. Energy work is not required by all aspects of Ceremonial Magick, in fact in a way it is its own practice. The Japanese practice known as Reiki also uses energy work on very similar principals as the energy work in magick. That said, trying very basic energy work is an excellent way for a beginner in Ceremonial Magick to not only perform magick, but also actually feel something physical to correspond to the practice.

To start, let us analyze friction in practice. Friction creates energy known as heat (9). We can create friction any time we want by simply rubbing our hands together. A variation of this exercise, as well as many other powerful exercises, can be found in Damien Echol's book "High Magick". "High Magick" has been a strong inspiration for quite a few exercises in this text. This book is another excellent resource for Ceremonial Magick that is strongly recommended. This exercise will incorporate a physical element with the visualization exercise from the previous chapter.

Friction Exercise

For this exercise you may find a comfortable place to sit, stand, or even lay down, and then you are free to begin:

1. Place your palms together. Begin to rub them together rapidly until you feel them become warm.

2. Separate your palms and begin to observe the transfer of energy. You will notice as they separate the warmth doesn't go away but instead exists between the gap in your hands. As you separate them further you will notice the heat dissipates further. The further you go the more the heat will dissipate until it is completely gone. This is because you are adding more air and distance between the original energy source until it eventual transfers out into another form of energy as the heat dissipates. Try this from step one a few times before moving on. It may seem silly, but try rubbing your hands faster or slower. Even try rubbing them for longer or shorter periods of time. Really examine and think about how it feels as you draw your hands closer and farther apart each time.

3. Once you are familiar with this sensation, close your eyes and rub your hands together again just like before.

4. Now as you separate your hands try to visualize the heat you feel as a ball of yellow light.

5. Once you can see the ball of light, try separating your hands further and visualize it expanding until it eventually dissipates and disappears.

6. Repeat steps 3 through 5 a few times until this visualization is familiar to you.

7. Now just like before, rub your hands together with your eyes closed. This time you are going to attempt to manipulate the energy. Don't worry if it doesn't feel quite right the first time, remember this is called an exercise for a reason.

8. As you separate your hands see the ball of light glow brighter and brighter but don't let it dissipate.

9. Bring your hands back together slowly and compress the ball of light. As you do so pay attention to how the heat feels. Analyze whether or not it is heating up again, or if it has dissipated already.

10. If it is dissipating see if you can heat it back up again without rubbing your hands together. Do this by focusing on the ball of light and remembering how the heat felt before. If the heat is growing see if you can make it hotter or colder by similar means of expanding the light or compressing it further.

11. Repeat steps 7 through 10 like before until you are able to exert some sort of control over the energy created by the friction. Remember you created this energy kinetically by rubbing your hands together. The energy is real and it is there. In fact you have successfully demonstrated how one can convert the work of kinetic energy into thermal energy, you just can't see it. Even though you can't see it, you can still feel it. Feeling it allows you to anchor your visualization to something physical. Using that connection you should be able to at least observe change, if not some small amount of control, via physical movements.

Congratulations you just did magick! Practice this exercise over and over again until the feeling and visualizations become easier to you. This exercise, while simple, can help you really hone in energetic and visualization skills that will help you immensely in later practices.

Water Exercise

For this exercise pour yourself a small glass of water and find a comfortable space to work with it. The water can be any temperature you prefer just make sure it is comfortable and safe to touch with your skin.

1. Place one finger in the water and soak it for a few seconds.
2. Remove your finger from the water and pay attention to how it feels. It likely feels wet, perhaps cold or warm depending on the temperature.
3. Take the wet finger and press it to another finger or even another part of your body where there is bare skin.
4. Pay attention to how that feels. Some of the moisture should now be physically present on the new surface and the temperature will have changed based on the temperature of the water and your finger.
5. Now, close your eyes and do the exact same thing as before. Dip your finger into the water.
6. Before you touch the other surface of your skin visualize your finger as being surrounded by white light wherever you feel the water.
7. As you touch the finger to the new surface of skin, see the white light begin to transfer to the new surface as you feel the physical properties of the skin change.
8. Repeat steps 5 through 7 as many times as you like. Try transferring it even further if you can. For example maybe transfer from one finger to the next until no further change is observable.

You have done magick yet again, congratulations! These exercises may seem a bit odd, but they have immense value when it comes to being able to practically observe what you are doing. Especially for those who have seldom worked in any realm of spirituality, this makes magick tangible by pairing it with basic physics. In essence if you remove the visualization, all you are doing is transferring energy, primarily the temperature from heat, or lack there of. This may seem like common sense, but in a way, so is magick. Everything in magick operates on tangible, practical formulas. This is an exact representation of that idea at a basic level. When you incorporate the visualization techniques you are now able to begin practicing control.

When it comes to control you may have noticed something. That is a limitation based on the energy source. When it came to friction, the distance between your hands and the air around you will always eventually dissipate the heat no matter how long you maintain it. Even with focus and practice to maintain it longer it will eventually always transfer as it is meant too. With water it's even more obvious. The energy from the air around you will eventually cool and dry the water, ultimately transferring it to a new temperature, and eventually a new state of energy. This is because the energy sources you are working with here are natural and abide by the laws of the universe. When you work with magick however, there are no more limitations. You move on from using natural phenomena to tapping into the perpetual motion machine itself that is the universe. That said, working with natural phenomena is just as much doing magick as tapping into the universe. This is where concepts between Ceremonial Magick and

Natural Magick are often shared. When it comes to energy work the idea is mostly the same. The difference later on will be Natural Magick focuses more on the properties of nature, as well as more physical items such as the natural elements, herbs, crystals, and even physical interactions between these sorts of tools. Ceremonial Magick does make heavy use of elements in nature, but at a level that is far less physical. If you do choose to use physical elements as tools, these Natural Magick items can help direct focus by making a given practice more tangible.

You are now a magickian, but before you start learning ritual work, it's important to practice control over your mind. The next chapters shall prepare you for the standard practices that you will eventually use every single day should you keep this up. Continue to practice these basic energy work exercises at least twice a day, if not more. They will help prepare you to feel the physical experiences that will go hand in hand with meditation as well as magick. Feel free to up your practice to repeat the exercises as many times as you can a day. Doing magick is not like doing physical exercise. Though at times you may need to rest, you do not exhaust yourself the same way you would doing a physical exercise. Pay attention to how you feel and rest when you need to, but in general the more you perform any practice or exercise in regards to magick, the faster you will progress.

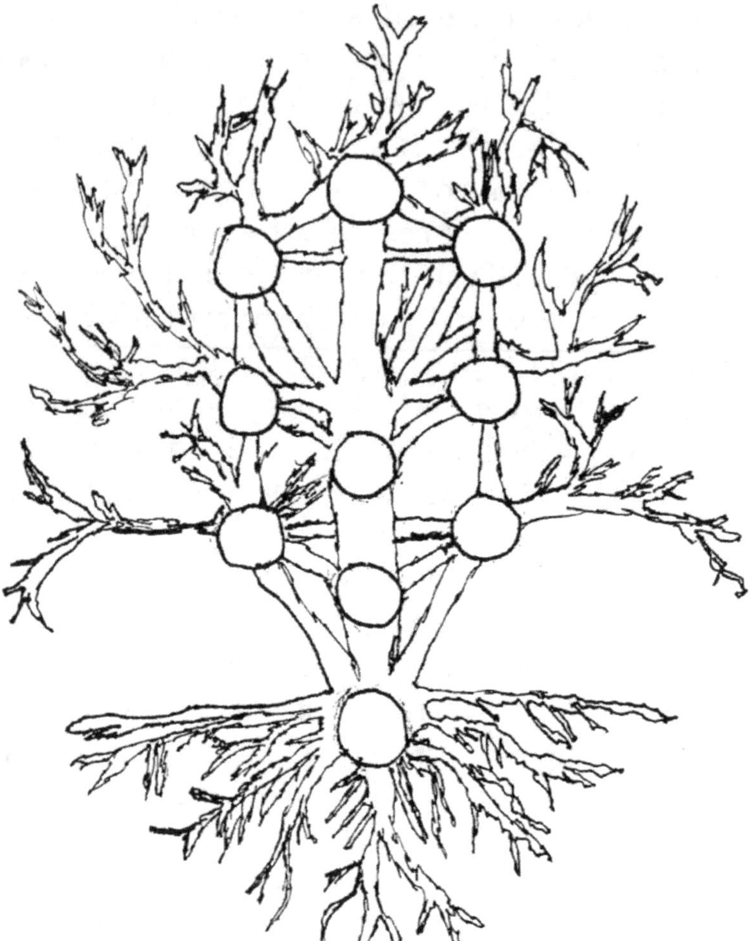

Tree of Life - Artistic Representation

Chapter 4: Meditation

Meditation practices come in all shapes and sizes. Different meditations have various purposes to help people achieve various states of mind. When it comes to magick, meditation is not necessarily a requirement, however it is essential in order to establish a baseline of understanding if you do ritual work. With Ceremonial Magick specifically, it is necessary as it is a meditative practice. As you may imagine it could be very difficult to focus on an intricate ritual if you can't clear you mind before beginning. At minimum meditation is a great practice to help one do exactly that, clear one's mind. On a personal note, I didn't even begin practicing magick outside of basic energy work until I completed years of meditation. Does this mean you'll have to do the same for years before progressing? Absolutely not, but it is worth considering spending a vast amount of time on before beginning. Ultimately it is my opinion that you can practice all of these meditations over the course of two months, dedicating two weeks to each. Once you do this you should be more than prepared to begin practicing Ceremonial Magick fully. That said, the longer you practice meditating, the easier things will come to you as you progress. More than that, keep in mind your brain is your own. It may take more or less time than someone else to get where you want to be. Don't rush it, take as long as is necessary for your mind.

Another teaching I've learned from listening to Jason Louv is to essentially keep meditation and magick separate. This may be confusing to conceptualize at first since Ceremonial Magick is a very "meditative" type of practice. That said, while it is very reminiscent of, and even dependent in some ways, on the same skills used by meditation, it is simply not a full meditation only practice at the end of the day. You do not want to be practicing full blown Zazen or even a Mindfulness meditation while you are focusing on Ceremonial Magick. That doesn't mean you can't meditate ever again, far from it. In fact I still do every day. There are even meditations taught by Ceremonial Magick that help one interact with different energies. However, those practices are part of Ceremonial Magick, where as something even as simple as Mindfulness is a practice on its own. You will want to put all your focus into whichever practice is your priority. If you are working on meditation, don't do Ceremonial Magick, or at least if you do keep it very simple. If you are working on Ceremonial Magick, you can still meditate, but be sure to do it inside of your magick practice. Make sure that the magick is the focus, not the meditation. Basically, put your focus into growing one and use the other as a side tool, or not at all. Don't try to grow both at once because often these are two paths to the same goal and if you don't focus singularly on one, you may never achieve the goals set by both. That said, try them all and if meditation works best for you perhaps that is a wise path to try, remember it's your journey!

Mindfulness

I've mentioned two meditation practices so far, both of which will be covered by this text. This section will introduce "Mindfulness", a very modernized meditation practice. In fact you may have heard of Mindfulness before. It has become a very mainstream meditation practice. Even modern software applications and companies like "Headspace" exist providing full blown courses to teach the practice. The goal of Mindfulness is in the name of the practice. It's a very simple, but very powerful practice that allows one to be more mindful and in control of one's thoughts, and by proxy, one's actions in life. Even though it is simple, do not be deceived, it is not necessarily easy. This is the practice I focused on for years before even entertaining other meditations, much less Ceremonial Magick. By doing so, other meditations were easy to dive into, and maintaining focus doing magick came naturally. Mindfulness could be considered the most fundamental meditation process as it gives you all the tools you need to do almost any other meditation practice without starting totally from scratch.

You can use any material you would like to learn mindfulness, as starting slow may be more beneficial than what is taught in this text. There are many resources out there for it, no matter what you use as a reference, what is awesome is you won't need the reference for very long. Of course following the text set forth is recommended, but it is encouraged to always broaden your resources if this practice appeals to you. Below three different exercises will be detailed. Each will be a stepping stone to the next, so master each one carefully before moving forward. Keep in mind, this practice is deceptively simple. Even from exercise to exercise it should be very clear how they build on one another. That said, it does not mean you won't be met with adversity or confusion. Just because something is clear does not mean it is easy to understand. In fact ponder on the clearest object you can think of for a moment. In a way you will likely see right through it. If you see through something you might just miss what that thing actually is. Do not be discouraged, remember if this stuff was easy, everyone would do it. Start here and grow!

1. Find some place to sit comfortably. Once you are there focus your attention on whatever is directly in front of you.
2. Begin to take slow deep breaths. Not heavy breaths but just deep enough that you feel them so they are physically noticeable.
3. Over time slowly begin to close your eyes. Take your time with this, let them close naturally after coaxing them to close at first.
4. Once your eyes are closed begin to pay attention to your breathing. Ask questions like, "How does it feel?", or "Is the breath sharp or fluid.", "Is it warm or cold?". Really take some time to focus on what is happening while you are breathing.
5. Over time begin to focus on just the physical actions of breathing. On each breath acknowledge and focus on the fact that you are simply either breathing in or out.
6. Sit still and focus on the breath for as long as you can. If you feel your mind start to wander then try and draw you attention back to the breath.

7. When you are ready to end simply gradually open your eyes. Once they are open take a moment to recognize how your body feels once it resumes being exposed to physical stimuli again.

This exercise is deceptively simple. You essentially just sit and focus on breathing for as long as you can. The challenge for many of us, if not all, is our minds are always thinking. We are just unaware of the thoughts. When you force focus like this you are taking control of your awareness again. It is often apparent that many people's brains might be trying to retake that focus to give attention to natural background thinking. All of this is normal, but at the end of the day it is your mind. Therefore you should get to decide when, and how, you want to think whether it is about foreground or background thoughts. Here are some tools to help with maintaining focus while performing a Mindfulness meditation practice.

1. **Noting:** This is the process of allowing thoughts to come through, but without actually thinking about them. We acknowledge them for a brief moment, but we purposely don't dive into further details of the thought. This allows you to essentially pass along your focus briefly and return the majority of it back to what it is you want to focus on. In the case of this meditation it would be back to the breath. You can even make actual mental notes that are a sort of a quick judgment of an incoming thought. You can note it by acknowledging what it is and then thinking about if you would label the thought "good" or "bad". A thought could be good for any number of reasons to you. Same as any thought that

seems bad to you could be bad for any number of reasons. It is based on whatever your first reaction is to the thought. Doing so makes sure you are aware of the thought and have at least prepared for yourself, regardless if it is a thought you look forward to having or not. This way you can let it go and choose to think about it later. Because you are now aware of the thought, you are in control. You can now decide that the present moment isn't the time to give it your full attention.

2. **Analyzing other physical movements:** Actively move your focus around to different things you feel in your body. Swap from the breath, to the heartbeat, to how your eyes feel closed. Examine your arms and fingers just based on how the feel where they are. Ask your self things like, "do they feel sore, relaxed, warm, or cold?. Simply identify different properties and feelings that your body is creating on its own without your intervention. Continually focus on each aspect as long or short as you want. This technique will help those that may have a mind that needs to be thinking of many things at once. We can still allow ourselves to do that, but we need to be in total control of what it is we actually want to think about, even when shifting focuses.

3. **Body scanning:** This is the process of thinking about how your body feels in a focused and purposeful way. It helps ground you in being present so you can maintain your focus, but in a more structured manner. Starting from your head at the very top, ask your self how it feels. What sensations are you experiencing in that area of your body? Any thoughts or keywords come to mind? Answer those kinds of questions for yourself as you are meditating. Only analyze it for a few moments, if you

find yourself losing track of a sense of time try to pace yourself to continue scanning every 10 seconds or so from the start. As you go scan down each section of your body:

1. Head
2. Neck
3. Shoulders
4. Right Arm
5. Left Arm
6. Chest
7. Stomach
8. Hips and Pelvis
9. Thighs
10. Calves
11. Ankles
12. Top of Feet
13. Toes
14. Bottom of Feet

You can also go in reverse order if you would like to start from the bottom of your body to the top instead. This exercise can also be done standing if you don't want to sit or lay down per the normal guidance. Do this over and over again until your meditation is complete. You could also use this as your own meditation timer. This means the scanning is done after going down and then back up the body. Depending on your pacing, you could make the last check be when it reaches your head again. After which, you may begin to open your eyes and conclude the meditation.

Once you feel comfortable start a timer to go with it. Go in increments of 5. Start with 5 minutes on the first day, 10 minutes on the second day, 15 minutes on the third day, 20 minutes on the fourth day 25 minutes on the fifth day, 30 minutes on the fifth day, etc...

If you do this for two weeks you will eventually end up with meditating in a 70 minute session. From here you can keep this up at the same increments daily until you decide to stop. Eventually this would have you end up in a 24/7 always meditating state, which is unrealistic to achieve if your focus is magick, or living out another part of your path in life. In theory if you just did that you'd have achieved the goal of magick and other meditations, but there's no way to really know from the outside looking in, as anyone who is teaching about mindfulness obviously isn't meditating every waking moment. If they were they couldn't speak, or write books. If that were the case, then we may not even know about mindfulness at all. However, it is worth acknowledging that doing so constantly would end up being a particular completion for this singular path. It would certainly cause some sort of deep introspection and growth, just with many practical consequences that arise naturally from essentially giving up life entirely to meditate until you are dust.

So keep it up for as long as you would like even as you do Ceremonial Magick, but remember at some point you have to recognize if you're more focused on a meditation practice rather than just using the tools learned from it in Ceremonial Magick. If so, then you may have a different path outgrowing your interest in any magick. This meditation would infinitely progress to having no practical time for anything else at all, much less magick. This may seem semantic and obvious to dig into, but it is this sort of detail that really illustrates the idea that there are many different paths to achieve the same thing. We don't know exactly what the experience is at the end of any it for sure, but we do know it is something we can't comprehend or experience in this state. If it were we'd have something better to relate it with. In this day and age there's not many better terms to really truly judge something as "good" or "bad" in a matter of fact. It's all opinion, because of the very fact that two different people could think, in the same situation, that something is both good *and* bad at the same time. For example if a person who likes bitter things thinks something is bitter, then they think that's good. While a person who does not like bitter things would think something that is bitter is bad.

So which is it, is bitter bad, or good? Depends on the perspective. We cannot possibly comprehend whether any end goal is good or bad, but through these practices we control our end goal. In this way we won't necessarily know if any end goal is good or bad, but rather that it *is*, and it is correct and complete. With completing a path of any sort, this means that the end goal is simply inevitable and it will happen to all energy at some point in time infinitely. We are simply taking control of experiencing that entire journey how we want, not just standing unaware.

All of these meditations, as well as Ceremonial Magick itself, will help you live life how you want to live it. You will be who you want to be by whatever definition that means to you. Do note, while you may be in control, it was only by training your mind to do what you want it do. Some of these paths lead to singular thinking patterns that allow for reduction of the physical needs to connect to the spiritual needs. Ceremonial Magick recognizes that all sources of energy, both physical and practical of the earth, all the way to the highest peak of conscious, focus, and thought within the brain. These two energies are all made of the same source. The physical ground beneath you right now was made from the same energy that causes the series of events that is responsible the creation of humanity. At one point that included your creation. Your thoughts and consciousness are the most physical concepts of what we can note as a spiritual comparison, because beyond these terms, spirituality is a unique experience that has no other truly consistent words per individual.

We use this placeholder term of spirituality for the realities we experience that are slightly higher than our own consciousness. We know they are there when we experience them, but have no clue what to call them, so spirituality stuck. All the thoughts we have, all the way up the chain to all the spiritual experiences we have, are all ultimately also a physical cause. This is precisely why we can orient ourselves and redirect energy to cause change in our lives.

Thanks to the laws of the universe that we've been able to reverse engineer thus far, it can be understood then that the concepts we experience labeled as spirituality are very physical and very real. This means we can interact with them via energy exchanges. We also know that different situations produce different kinds of energy exchange. We map these formulas to express precisely how a given exchange of energy works. Just like the kinetic energy of friction produces the thermal energy of heat via a specific set of exchange rules that maintain a law of physics. This means that in order to express change, we have to cause reactions via specific formulas that cause a change at a physical and meta-physical level.

Meditation practices are one powerful, yet simple, example of how someone can take over their destiny by simply existing. That is the base formula, exist and be. That formula is capable of cause immense change that you specifically created for yourself. Ceremonial Magick is another powerful, but more intricately defined, and focused practice, to accelerate what meditative practices also do. It is nice to have clear options of simplicity and no gimmicks. These provide a clear, logical, outcome of how those events of change may be physically observable as fact. Part of a good practice in magick is acknowledging that the formulas are far more intricate, and correspond to many detailed things. If you chase the rabbit hole too far down you'll never quite come back up as you'll reach something infinite in the source itself.

It's good to learn the deeper mechanics, but remember, the real benefit comes from doing them. It doesn't matter if you understand every intricate detail and correspondence of each archangel, and their corresponding angel counterparts, that you're supposed to just murmur names and air draw symbols for in a meditative state. Especially if you've never physically done it. That sounds silly, because it is. Unless you are simply learning the history of magick, knowing these practices by heart does nothing for you if you never do them. That said, be skeptical, reverse engineer many rituals, but don't get lost in it. The knowledge you can gain from learning how Ceremonial Magick works in a fuller context is so that you can create your own path since you'll have a stronger idea of how it all truly functions.

The reason we can get a strong idea is because everything in magick is based on a stepping stone that was built up higher one step at a time. While some stones were different shapes and sizes, they were all stepping stones meant to sit atop one another. If you can lift one stone, you can lift all the stones, you just may only be able to do it based on how many stones you can physically lift at a time. If you decide you don't like one stone, you can go find other stones, or even try to make something that is equivalent to a given stone that works for you. It is all about what you can carry, both physically and metaphorically. It is precisely what makes it possible for a magickian to create a ritual that is so simple requiring something like the wink of an eye, yet causes vast amounts of focused, purposeful change. They just figured out the formula needed to cause the shift in energy and decided to carry that metaphorical stone in this context.

This whole stone metaphor is simply a parallel to the fundamental concept of knowledge. Knowledge is gained, stored, and reused by our conscious mind. You get knowledge by learning. Picking up a stone is learning. You may find that you can pick up many stones, or perhaps even create a stone that represents every possible stone in time. Doing the latter would imply that you have every stone without carrying every stone, just one that holds the energy of all. This is equivalent to storing permanent knowledge. As we learn we often only juggle one or two things at a time. Once we've understood something, we will retain it and remove the weight to be able to make room for something new. If you really think about it, carrying too many stones is another way to say you don't know something, or anything yet. If once you learned it, you can put down, restructure, and replace the stone, then you shouldn't be carrying all the weight of as many stones over time. Carrying less stones means you have acquired knowledge. So in order to cause change, we need to know how to make change. Energy exchange is the physics answer for how that works (2), but spiritual practices are just another set of mechanics for influencing that change.

Prison Cell Meditation

Prison cell meditation is another technique taught in Damien Echols's book High Magick. It is another incredibly powerful and simple meditation technique that actually incorporates a little bit of passive energy work. I have modified it a little to address some challenges that one may run into when being unaware of what sensations they need to be causing themselves to experience. In essence you will simply be sitting down and visualizing a cold dark prison cell around you with one window for light. You'll have to imagine yourself climbing the wall and your goal is to briefly immerse yourself in the bright light from the windows over and over again.

1. Find some place to sit comfortably. Once you are there focus your attention on whatever is directly in front of you.
2. Begin to take slow deep breaths. Not heavy breaths but just deep enough that you feel them and so they are noticeable.

3. Over time slowly begin to close your eyes. Take your time with this, let them close naturally after coaxing them to close at first.

4. Once your eyes are closed visualize a prison cell around you. Ideally you'll want to see grey concrete floors, ceilings, and walls. No beds, no furniture. Just four walls, and you. One of the walls has a small window with white light peaking through.

5. Begin to notice everything you visualize in as great a detail as possible. Try incorporating physical memories that relate to the visualization. Think about what it feels like to sit on the concrete if you have before, and really focus on it. Try to feel it again as part of the visualization. If you are having a hard time visualizing and feeling these elements because the imagery isn't clear to you, simply try and come up with what an equivalent prison would be for you. As long as it is a physical room that is darkened, and only light pours through a single small window, or small hole in the wall. No other doors, windows, furniture, or exits should be present, but the aesthetic of the room can be anything that is easy for you to visualize.

6. After visualizing yourself sitting for a bit, try to make yourself get up and climb to view out of the tiny window. Don't actually physically move, but in your visualization see yourself climb the wall and begin to peer out the window into the bright white light.

7. Let the light wash over you, fill the room behind you, and be all that you see until you are surrounded by infinite bright blinding light.

8. After a few moments return back to the cell floor and see everything become dark again with the only light peering from the window.

9. Repeat steps 1 through 8 as many times as you possibly can before you lose focus. Try to add more repetitions to it each time you meditate. Optionally you can just make it time based. For example start out with 10 minutes of the meditation being purposefully dedicated to visualizing being immersed in the light after looking through the window, and then 5 minutes of sitting on the cell floor. The goal here is to visualize the light over and over again as much as possible. With the more repetitions you do, you will naturally be surrounding yourself with more light.

10. When you are ready to end simply gradually open your eyes. Once they are open take a moment to recognize how your body feels being exposed to physical stimuli again. If you need a physical cue lightly clap your hands, snap your fingers, or tap your foot to regain focus.

This meditation practice is designed to begin building your energy and aura. The aura is simply a term used to describe what holds our energy. It's not visible normally because it doesn't really do anything on its own. The external world and our own actions do things to it. In this case we are drawing in white light as an idea that will convert to energy in our minds, therefore producing a thought. This is the formula for forcing a specific thought. In this case we are bringing white light that represents "the source" of divine energy. Generally this just brings us closer to our true will, and is a fantastic goto representation of energy. If you're ever unsure what other correspondences to use when visualizing light, this type light covers all of them. Doing this practice over and over again is a really good way to get used to experiencing that light in terms of visualization skills. Additionally you'll actually be doing analysis and experiencing the change that occurs as you perform the meditation.

Seasonal Meditation

Seasonal meditation is the process of meditating on the four seasons of Spring, Summer, Fall, and Winter. Seasonal meditation is called many things from "Meditating on the Four Seasons" to "Changing Seasons Meditation", but ultimately you can kind of see it's just semantics of saying the exact same thing. It is even taught as a more advanced Mindfulness practice by some teachers, but some variation of this exercise is observable in almost any meditative practice that exists. As you can see, the names aren't all that different, no matter what practice teaches it. The change of seasons is a commonly corresponding to a representation of the cycle of life. Often things begin to grow and come to life in the Spring, thrive in the Summer, slowly rest or begin to recede in the Fall, completely die by Winter, and then the cycle repeats. By immersing ourselves in the experience of the changing seasons, we more deeply experience the natural cycle of life. Seasonal meditation has many benefits in Ceremonial Magick. First off it helps you become even more comfortable with visualizations as it is a very visualization heavy exercise. It also provides the benefit of becoming familiar with how your physical and mental senses interact with those visualizations by requiring you to actually experience the change of seasons. During the meditation you will feel and see yourself experience sensations from each season. Once you become accustomed to each one, you can choose to just focus on one season at at time instead of all at once. Some people enjoy meditating on each season during that given season and only transitioning during the natural change of seasons. Since we are building skills for Ceremonial Magick, at first you should focus on experiencing all four during each session. This will help strengthen visualizations even further for later exercises.

1. Find some place to sit comfortably or lie down. Once you are there focus your attention on whatever is directly in front of you.
2. Begin to take slow deep breaths. Not heavy breaths but just deep enough that you feel them so they are noticeable.
3. Over time slowly begin to close your eyes. Take your time with this, let them close naturally after coaxing them to close at first.
4. Once your eyes are closed inhale to the count of four.
5. Hold your breath to the count of four and begin to visualize a Spring setting. This can be anything, but make sure it makes you feel and focus on what Spring means to you as a season. It can be as simple as visualizing a sunflower, all the way to imagining yourself sitting in a meadow, imagining a light warmth on your skin and scents of honey. You may also want to try

experiencing rain during this season, try to visualize and really feel what the rain feels like on your skin, and then as the sun comes out, feel the warmth.

6. Exhale to the count of four and continue to experience the visualization of Spring.

7. Hold the exhaled breath again to the count of four and begin to see the Spring season change to Summer.

8. With Summer try to feel the warmth of the sun. Maybe feel stronger sensations of heat, or see more flowers and trees produced from the Spring. Just like before inhale for four, hold for four, exhale for four, and hold for four. You will do this type of breathing throughout the entire exercise. It is known as the "Four Fold Breath". This breathing style will be used in many exercises later, and will be addressed again, but for now simply follow along.

9. As you hold your exhaled breath again transition from Summer to Fall. Visualize things like the leaves turning brown and falling from trees around you. Perhaps the air is getting colder, and smells of autumn like pumpkins or spices are noticeable. Continue the Four Fold Breath pattern the same way as before.

10. Once again as you hold the exhaled breath visualize a transition from Fall to Winter. Feel the air become cold, imagine snow falling. Think of smells of Winter holidays like gingerbread, or perhaps pine trees. Continue the Four Fold Breath pattern once again.

11. Now you may repeat steps 4 through 10 over and over as many times as you like. If you do so, be sure to transition between Winter and Spring. See the snow melt and begin to focus on the sensations of Spring again as you hold the exhaled breath. Try to do this for

as long as you can. There is no hard and fast rule on when to stop. That said, do try to repeat this over and over through all four seasons for at least 10 minutes every day. Attempt to increase as you go until it is like second nature to you.

12. When you are ready to end simply gradually open your eyes, and once they are open take a moment to recognize how your body feels being exposed to physical stimuli again. If you need a physical cue lightly clap your hands, snap your fingers, or tap your foot to regain focus like always.

From here feel free to try just meditating on one season at a time and immerse yourself deeper in the visualization. The way to do this is by simply observing the steps taught previously, but instead of transitions to other seasons, on each hold of the exhaled breath try to strengthen the visualization and sensations you feel regarding the season you are focused on. This exercise is very immersion driven, and requires a lot of focus. The use of seasons and their changes is used not only because it is something familiar that we almost all have a reference to, but it also makes us feel more present by focusing on the natural world around us. By the time you have mastered this practice it is likely you not only will be more in tune with seasonal changes, but also have identified a new love for a season you may have disliked. In time this not only improves your visualization skills, but also your understanding of the natural cycle of life represented by the changing of seasons. You can take this even further by meditating outside in nature to get a more tactile sensation for a given season that is occurring at that time. There is a lot of room for experimentation and growth with this exercise alone. Once you feel comfortable in it, your ability to visualize will hopefully have improved drastically. This is a very simple way to observe complex visualizations during meditation.

Zazen Meditation

Zazen is another simple mindfulness practice. Zazen is a Japanese meditation practice taught by Zen Buddhism practices (3). The form taken for this meditation is to put a cushion on the floor and kneel on the cushion. You will be sitting on the heels of your feet as you kneel, and you will want to place your hands in your lap with your palms up. Your hands should be laid one on top of the other with thumbs touching. A visual representation of this form is shown below.

Zazen Form - Visual Representation

If you are unable to practice in the traditional form that is perfectly fine, simply make yourself comfortable like you did in the other exercises and follow the rest of the steps.

1. Once you are ready to begin, keep your eyes open and focus on the floor directly in front of you. Try to look a couple of feet ahead of you but maintain direct focus on the floor. If you are modifying this simply focus on whatever is a few feet ahead of you at the present moment. You will keep your eyes open the entire time, but you may notice that your physical focus in sight will lessen as your mind focuses on other aspects.
2. Breathe normally and notice the breath at first.
3. Now begin to pay attention to your body. How does your head feel, what about your hands and feet, or your stomach? Notice the air, is it flowing in or out currently? How do your breaths feel, are they shallow or deep?
4. The important thing from here on is to continue to notice every little thing about your body *without* making any judgement calls or thinking about it in any detail. Especially if you are in the traditional form, you will notice your body begins to physically hurt. Your feet and spine will likely become weary or sore. Your goal is to not think about if the feelings you are observing are good or bad, but just notice what they are. Label them and gradually move along to another part of your body.
5. When experiencing particularly painful, or even positive, sensations during this practice it can be easy to lose focus. That's okay, if you notice you are over thinking or not focusing on your body anymore, simply acknowledge that you lost focus and return to the body. Try to pick a new spot to resume your focus on.

6. Continue to hold this focus for as long as you can. Start
   off with 5 minutes of this exercise and gradually increase
   that time as you get used to it. With the traditional form
   this will be physically difficult to maintain at first, so
   start slow. As you do this exercise more and more it will
   become easier to sit for longer periods of time.
7. When you are ready to end simply stand up slowly and
   regain your physical focus.

Zazen is essentially just Mindfulness Meditation with extra focus. If you were to dive into a Mindfulness practice you would later be taught to do the "body scan" that was mentioned in the Mindfulness Meditation section of this text. This is essentially what you do the entire time you meditate in the style of Zazen. The primary difference between the two is that Mindfulness has no strict form, and body scanning is usually taught in a specific way (going up and down your body gradually over and over), as opposed to just setting your focus where you see fit based on what you notice.

The sitting form you take with Zazen requires you to deal with a physical element of pain that will distract you at first. While this is true, it is also a powerful tool to reset and maintain your focus by giving your body something to feel, and focus your attention on. Even if you're doing a modified version that requires less physical strain, you will still be able to observe the ultimate purpose of this meditation if you set your focuses correctly.

That purpose is to be present, observe the current moment, and your existence therein. Not only that, but you also do so without thinking or passing judgement. You begin to simply exists, and that is the goal.

Meditation - Artistic Representation of Meditation in nature

Chapter 5: Rituals

Rituals have been around likely since the dawn of time. It simply depends on how you define what a ritual is. At the base level a ritual is synonymous to a regular habit that you do, or a daily routine. In the context of a spiritual practice however, rituals are more like a set of purposeful, focused instructions that have a specific outcome. Whether you do a ritual for simple reverence, celebration, cleansing, or to accomplish something often you are doing a very precise set of things to fulfill that end goal. Rituals are very common in religious practices, as mentioned previously in this text. Even using modern Christianity as an example, we can see that this tradition follows very heavy ritual practices. A few examples of a Christian ritual practice would be:

✦ Mass - A group worship that celebrates the sacrament of the Eucharist.

✦ Baptism - An often water based ritual that cleanses and regenerates the baptized. Often used as a rite of passage in formally joining a church or to proclaim one's faith in the context of Christianity.

✦ Marriage Ceremonies - Specific gatherings to proclaim and affirm the union of two individuals by blessing it in the eyes of God.

✦ Prayer - Prayer is just meditation and manifestation, but in the context of Christianity, you focus entirely on a singular all powerful God related to Christian theology.

All of these things could be considered exoteric Ceremonial Magick practices that are currently observed by most Christian churches. In fact you could incorporate these into your Ceremonial Magick practice, especially if you identify with that faith. The difference between these exoteric practices and the more esoteric practices being taught by this text, is just that. One is actively taught, encouraged, and practiced by large modern communities. The others are lesser known and not adopted by those same communities. This is why esoteric practices often get lost in time if they are not kept up with.

Rituals can fall in and out of exoteric or esoteric status simply with the change of time and communities. Conserving knowledge of what is real and works is crucial to keeping Ceremonial Magick alive as a practice. For this reason the Christian Bible might be considered one of the greatest books of Ceremonial Magick that exists. That's why it is even relevant to mention this religion in the context of Ceremonial Magick to begin with. Once you begin to read the rituals and teachings of the Christian Bible from the perspective of being a Magickian, you may start to see the greater point to it all. You may even choose to incorporate some of the practices that are observed by modern Christian churches because they might work well for your path. Reading other religious texts are also strongly encouraged of course if that is of interest. Once your perspective is shifted to interpreting things through the lens of being a Ceremonial Magickian, you will begin to see patterns, rituals, and deeper meaning in many exoteric and esoteric texts. In reality magick is a constant. It cannot be emphasized enough that simply existing, and contributing to your own life in a natural way, is also magick. You're doing it right now, the difference between simply existing and adopting a practice is the intention, focus, and goal.

In comparison, some LaVeyan Satanist actually practice many of the same rituals that Christians and Ceremonial Magickians do. This is a perfect contrast between two seemingly opposing traditions, to emphasize how important broadening ones understanding across different spiritual paths can be. There are more similarities than one might think, and is exactly why these two religions were chosen as examples. Some samples of these practices would be:

+ Le Messe Noire (Black Mass): This the same thing in essence as the Christian Mass, but instead the group recites various chants of worship to honor themselves and Satan.

+ Baptism: In baptism performed by Satanist groups the goal could be seen as a reverse of purification. The goal in this ritual is to introduce and enforce the idea of "original sin" rather than cleanse and remove it. If you follow this path though, then this could be considered a cleansing for you all the same, it's subjective based on your worldview and beliefs.

+ Lesser Banishing Ritual of the Pentagram: This ritual is a banishing and cleansing ritual taught by Ceremonial Magick, and adapted to many other practices. In Satanism practitioners of this ritual call upon Satan, or even demons only, rather than working with angels. In Ceremonial Magick this can be done both ways, but often focuses on angelic magick in traditional teachings.

All world religions and practices incorporate magick in some way whether they call it that or not. Many see

Christianity and Satanism as direct opposing forces which makes using them as examples to demonstrate the influence of Ceremonial Magick interesting. You may think of some religions as exact opposites, but they all ultimately come from the same root, you just choose which branches to cling to on your path. The point here is that Ceremonial Magick is a powerful tool used all around the world even if it is not actively named as such.

What is the point of doing a ritual in Ceremonial Magick? Rituals are the fundamental formulas and building blocks of a Ceremonial Magick practice. They can be small acts like prayer or archangel meditation, all the way to elaborate rituals and ceremonies to produce a specific result. The ultimate goal of all of these smaller works is to achieve TGW. In fact one could only do a basic ritual all of their life and still achieve the same outcome as someone who has done something as complex as the somewhat infamous Abramelin Ritual. The caveat to this is doing only minor ritual work will likely take much, much longer compared to the more complex work. This is just by nature of the formulas. They all ultimately get you there, but if the goal is to achieve TGW in one life time then it was, and still is, important to accelerate that path as we learn more about how we can impact the universe with these practices.

One important thing to make note of is a practice known as "Chaos Magick". Chaos Magick is more of a mindset than a practice overall. Chaos Magickians incorporate practices from anything they deem useful. Often it still results in a lot of traditional Ceremonial Magick, but the mindset is focused on "what works and makes sense" rather than following strict formulas. Chaos Magickians may prefer a more scientific and psychological outcome rather than a focus on TGW. This is important to outline because when introducing Ceremonial Magick you may think modifying anything means you are now practicing Chaos Magick. This is simply not the case, the difference is the mindset.

A Chaos Magickian can strictly practice Ceremonial Magick in the most detailed and precise way and still achieve a different outcome based on what their goals are. Where as a practitioner focused on TGW is always doing Ceremonial Magick. That's not to say a Chaos Magickian wouldn't achieve TGW, they absolutely could if that's their focus. Chaos Magickians often have to put in even more effort at times to do things correctly, as modifying formulas requires understanding those formulas in a deeper way.

Chaos Magick is a beautiful thing, but it is not something recommended for a beginner. In general, sticking to a practice that leaves less room for error will result in more consistent success. That said, please do explore this concept of magick as you grow, as you should all others. There is nothing inherently negative about Chaos Magick at all. In fact, Jason Louv is a fantastic Chaos Magickian that has not only been mentioned, but has inspired many ideas in this text. He has been known to frequently use the mindset of a Chaos Magickian in his modern teaching, and has seen wondrous success among his students. It is simply important to understand that Chaos Magick is not what is being taught in this text, but modification in a stricter context will be. With that stated, the breaking down of concepts into digestible ideas is one thing this text does pull from Chaos Magick in admiration. This is to help provide accessibility to further the growth of Ceremonial Magick as a practice.

As previously stated, feel free to modify and change things as you see fit, but be sure you understand why and how to do so before you do. When it comes to beliefs and spirituality many may not feel comfortable with the Abrahamic focus that Ceremonial Magick naturally aligns with. I strongly encourage you to see past any religious bias and simply try it for yourself. If it works, begin to understand it, and if you still dislike working with it in the traditional manner, feel free to change it! Be sure to keep the spiritual focus in mind as you do these rituals. If you just wanted to manipulate things on a practical level, the traditional field of science outside of metaphysics and esotericism would be a better way to go. It is just as wonderful of a thing to get lost in and contribute to, the end goal is simply different. Just keep in mind without some level of openness to these abstract concepts, you are doing nothing more than self help, or worse, a botched version of Chaos Magick. None of these things are bad or wrong, simply put Ceremonial Magick is for one goal, while the other practices have other goals. This text teaches Ceremonial Magick, so set your expectations as you dive in to be prepared for the kind of change that has been outlined.

Four Fold Breath

You've already practiced the "Four Fold Breath" if you've completed the earlier meditation exercises. Here it will be outlined in greater depth so you may practice it before beginning the other rituals that require it. It may seem simple, but like with all things in Ceremonial Magick, making the fundamentals second nature will go a long way. The last thing you want to do is be distracted by your breathing while trying to manifest something specific. The breathing is a tool, and part of a formula, but it is not the focal point of any practice outside of common meditation. Once you can breathe in this pattern on demand and naturally, performing the upcoming rituals will be much easier.

1. Find someplace quiet to focus. You may sit, stand, lie down, or place yourself into any position that feels comfortable. Sitting or standing is recommended but it really doesn't matter as long as you can focus.
2. Close your eyes and begin to inhale. As you inhale count to four slowly. It doesn't have to be precise or very long, just long enough to feel calm and focused on the breath. Try to fill your lungs if you can.
3. Once you've finished inhaling, hold the same breath to the count of four the exact same way.
4. Release the breath and exhale to the count of four just like you have been. Try to empty your lungs of all the air that was inhaled.
5. Hold your breath again after exhaling and count to four one last time.
6. Done! You have completed the Four Fold Breath. Repeat steps 2 through 5 as much as you'd like. This in itself can help make one feel calmer, more focused, and is in fact a basic meditation if you incorporate the Mindfulness practice of focusing on the breath.

Keep in mind this breathing technique is just that, a technique. It is not meditation on its own, but as is mentioned in step 6 one can add on to the technique to create a meditative practice. Similarly we will add this technique to rituals going forward. As you'll see in the Lesser Banishing Ritual of the Pentagram later on, the Four Fold Breath isn't emphasized at all, only mentioned. That's because you'll be using that technique to naturally assist with transitions from step to step based on the breathing patterns. It's a useful tool for queues in a ritual as much as it is for general calmness and control over your breathing.

The Great Communicator - Artistic Representation of the Archangel Ambriel

Chapter 6: Grounding Exercises

Grounding is a term used throughout magickal practices, but also is a common term when working with electricity. Electricity is another form of energy. When controlling a current of electricity, a smart thing to do is implement a grounding wire. Grounding in this context gives the electricity another place to flow safely if for some reason the current is disrupted. This is exactly what is happening when you ground yourself in Ceremonial Magick, just on a spiritual level. Many rituals recommend you cleanse, or ground yourself, before you begin. This is because you are drawing in outside energy you want to control, and if you as a conduit have extra energy bouncing around, then you may disrupt the flow of what you intended to draw in.

Grounding also helps you feel "centered" and is often synonymous with the concept of centering ones self. This idea is basically creating a sense of wholeness, clarity, and peace within yourself. You force your focus to be present and aware so you can determine what happens next. There are a ton of ways to ground yourself. Many rituals for cleansing can even double as grounding rituals if they incorporate some grounding mechanism within their steps. Grounding on its own however can simply help you to reduce stress and maintain focus in life, even if you aren't preparing to do Ceremonial Magick.

It is extremely healthy and beneficial to take a pause and ground yourself as you go through your day. Doing so will often allow you to experience life more presently. Being present is not our default state as humans. We are always looking ahead to the next thing, or looking to our past and dwelling on it. What's in the future will always come, and what is in the past has happened. The past and future are both just time stamps of the present, at one point they were your present. This is why it's important to focus heavily on impacting the present moment as it is what controls everything in your life.

Walking Outside

The easiest thing you can do to ground yourself is simply going for a walk outside. Ideally you want to do this barefoot and physically touch the ground. You don't have to be out in nature, but the whole point is to get as close to the actual ground as possible. If all you have to work with is concrete in a city then that's more than good enough. Going to a quiet space, especially a forest, will have a stronger initial impact but ultimately use what you have access to, and it will all be the same. What is important is that you focus on connecting yourself to the ground and your surroundings. From here let your walking naturally ground your energy to the earth beneath you. Think of it as your body acting as a natural ground wire for transferring electricity, but instead it is your natural energy. The earth beneath you will naturally take anything stealing your focus and replace it with a focus of your surroundings in the present moment. As you walk you will begin to notice only what is around you, how the ground feels, and what sounds you hear. You'll no longer dwell on whatever thoughts you had prior. Once you notice that state of presence, you've successfully grounded yourself.

Of course this state of consciousness isn't permanent, but it will last some time after you complete your walk. The reality is once you stop focusing on grounding and resume your daily life, you will begin to be focused on new energies. You most assuredly will become distracted and engulfed with those energies once again. However, the more frequently you ground yourself, the easier it will be to regain focus even without doing an exercise for it. Familiarity with this state of grounded consciousness will be trained over time, allowing you to reset your state as you wish should you become distracted. This is one way to maintain focus in the present moment consistently throughout your lifetime.

Qabalistic Cross

The Qabalistic Cross is the first ritual you will learn in this text if following along in order. This is a ritual taught by traditional Ceremonial Magick and not only grounds you, but seals your aura for protection. With more complex rituals, conducting the Qabalistic Cross is often the first step. Memorize this one closely as it is extremely useful and will be repeated many times as you learn other techniques.

If you have ever been to a Christian church that practices the "sign of the cross" then you've already seen an example of the Qabalistic Cross ritual. The sign of the cross is just a simplified version of the same ritual. In fact doing it in this manner, even simplified, does exactly what the full version does. It blesses you, protects you, and seals your aura. So if you're ever in a pinch and don't have time to observe the full ritual, simply crossing yourself and adding in the verbiage taught in this text will prove quite effective. Of course it is not a replacement for doing the full ritual as you will be drawing less energy and focus, but it is fundamentally yielding a similar result.

Before you begin, understand that this will be the first introduction in this text to the more spiritual concepts taught by Ceremonial Magick. You will need to be open to the concept of visualizing "the source" of energy and speaking Hebrew mantras. In the context of most things in Ceremonial Magick when you are dealing with various external entities, even "the source", it is important to remain reverent. Treat these entities and concepts as divine. Don't worship them necessarily unless that's part of your own personal belief system, but rather respect and express some gratitude at minimum. You are basically commanding the whole of divinity to do your bidding, the least you can do is be respectful. It is the same idea with asking a friend to do something for you. Eventually, if you are just mean and condescending all the time, they may not want to work with you, even if they would anyway. This creates an unhealthy relationship within your own conscious and subconscious. Showing kindness and respect, or even love, will go a very long way.

In Ceremonial Magick you're trying to become just as whole and powerful as "the source" itself so you can return to it, and carry out your true will. As you continue you will ideally begin to recognize all of it as one and the same. It is simply a perspective shift, and if you treat these external representations poorly, you ultimately treat yourself poorly since that is what you're trying to become. Keep this in mind. It is unlikely anything crazy is going to happen by not doing so. The ground isn't going to split open before you and damn you to suffering or something silly like that, but you won't accomplish the goal of TGW that way. It is important to recognize you are in control, but always be kind and respectful. That is just generally decent life advice as well. The following steps outline how to conduct the Qabalistic Cross ritual.

1. If you are able, conduct this ritual standing with your arms at your sides. If not, sitting or laying down is fine, but standing is the traditional means this ritual is often conducted.
2. Close your eyes and take deep breaths. As you breathe in the next steps try using the Four Fold Breath technique.
3. As you inhale begin to visualize white light from the world around you coming in through your nose and filling up your body.
4. Once you've finished inhaling the white light, visualize an infinite bright white light above the very top of your head. Exhale naturally and continue the breathing pattern.

5. Visualize yourself in the room which you are standing and continue to inhale white light. As you inhale each time, begin to see your self grow larger within in the room.

6. Repeat step 5 until you visualize yourself growing so large that you are above the entire universe. This is a bit abstract, so one idea is to picture yourself physically growing above the earth, then above space, and continue until there is infinite blackness below you and infinite light above you.

7. Once you feel like you can't grow yourself any further, inhale and visualize yourself breaking into the white light that was previously above you. Feel and see yourself being surrounded by the bright white light until it is fully surrounding you and is all that you see.

8. Touch two fingers to your forehead and inhale again. Vibrate or chant the mantra *Ateh* (Ah-tay) anywhere from 3 to 5 times (or more if you'd like, there is no limit). Ateh is a Hebrew mantra for *"Thou Art"*.

   ✦ Vibration is a new concept here, but it's exactly what you might think it is. You are simply saying the words in a low, monotone voice. Almost like singing, but more in your chest. Simply speaking, chanting the words, or even singing them works too, but vibration is the traditional means so if you are able to, then do so.

9. Inhale and visualize yourself draw a white line of light from your forehead to your chest. See the light shoot vertically down the rest of your body all the way to the ground.

10. Just like step 8, touch your fingers to the center of your chest and inhale. As you exhale vibrate the mantra

Malkuth (Mal-kouth). *Malkuth* is a Hebrew mantra for "The Kingdom". As you repeat the mantra see the line of light you just drew down your body grow infinitely bright and infinitely long. This means as bright as you can make it, and see the light shoot both below and above you into the light surrounding you where it bleeds into your surrounds to no end.

11. Like you did in step 9, inhale and draw a horizontal line of white light, but now to your left shoulder.

12. Vibrate the mantra *Vegeburah* (Veh-geh-boo-rah) just like before, and see the light drawn to your left shoulder glow infinitely bright and become infinitely long extending from your shoulder to the left side of your surroundings. *Vegeburah* is a Hebrew mantra for *"The Power"*.

13. Once again inhale, and draw a line of white light to your right shoulder.

14. Vibrate the mantra *Vegehdula* (Veh-gey-do-lah) and see the line of light grow infinitely brighter and infinitely extend from your right shoulder. *Vegehdula* is a Hebrew mantra for *"The Glory"*.

15. At this point a brilliant cross made of infinite white light should be extending through your body and into the light around you. The cross portion of the ritual is now complete.

16. Fold your hands over your chest and vibrate the mantra *Le Olam Amen* (Lee oh-lom ah-men). As you do so visualize the entire cross growing infinitely brighter, even brighter than it already is. Try to see it get brighter with each vibration of the mantra. Even if you don't think you can make it more bright than it already is, keep trying until you've finished the mantra. *Le Olam* is

the Hebrew mantra for *"Forever"* and *Amen* is for *"So be it"*.

17. Open your eyes and let the visualizations all gradually fade away. Once they have, stomp your foot, snap your fingers, or clap your hands to signify the ritual is complete and solidify your present focus.

18. At this point you have basically crossed yourself and stated "Thou art the kingdom, the power, the glory, forever, so be it". In Christian traditions one might recite "In the name of the Father, the Son, and the Holy Spirit, amen", or even "For thine is the kingdom, the power, and the glory forever, amen". It is not too different from what is still observed in Christianity today, but the one difference is the focus. In the exoteric variation of the exercise taught by Christianity, the focus is on asking God for protection and praising God in worship. In the Qabalistic Cross you are still bringing down protection from God, or "the source" of divine energy, but you are bringing it into yourself. Essentially stating "bless me as this is *my* kingdom, power, and glory, forever, so be it". This is important because in Ceremonial Magick we are trying to unify and ground ourselves to be one with the source of all this energy. It is important to be reverent and acknowledge divinity still, otherwise this may seem blasphemous in terms of linguistics, but it is really anything but. The whole idea is to draw you closer to, and allow you to experience divinity in the way that will help you complete TGW and return to the source.

From here if you are in a pinch you may simply cross your self and recite *Ateh, Malkuth, Vegeburah, Vegehdula, Le Olam, Amen* to perform a simplified version of the

Qabalistic Cross at anytime, anywhere. This ritual as a whole will successfully draw in the purest, most divine energy, and seal your aura with it. The end result provides grounding in the divine, cleansing over your present aura, and protection so that no external forces can change that aura. This is a ritual you will use over and over again going forward. Be sure to practice often, multiple times a day if you can. You will want this to be natural and easy for you to execute as time goes on.

Grounding Meditation

Grounding Meditation is a meditation technique taught by some Ceremonial Magickians. It is not necessarily a ritual in and of itself, but it works a lot like one. This technique is extremely powerful for grounding oneself and is a fantastic precursor to a ritual known as "The Middle Pillar". This technique combines the benefits of being outside in nature (if you are able) with techniques of directing energy taught by Ceremonial Magick. This has the same end goal of grounding in general, but does so in an extremely powerful way.

1. Performing this Grounding Meditation is ideally done while standing, but it may also be performed while lying down. Ideally, if you are able to stand, going outside and standing barefoot as close to the earth as possible

will yield the most powerful result by incorporating the physical senses. This is not a requirement though, it can be just as effective standing inside of a quiet room as it would outside, you will simply not have as rooted of a physical element to assist you.

2. Close your eyes and relax your body.

3. Visualize a black sphere beneath your feet. The bottom half of the sphere should go below the earth underneath you or under the surface you're standing on. The top half should be above the ground and you should see yourself standing directly on top of it.

4. Inhale, as you do visualize energy from the universe around you as white light flowing into you. Direct this energy in a straight line of white light from the top of your head, straight down vertically until it reaches the black sphere at your feet.

5. Continue a four fold breath pattern. As you inhale each time imagine fire growing through and out of the black sphere you are standing on.

6. Continue growing the flames, try to see them grow large enough to engulf your feet. Try to feel the flames on your feet. Make them feel hot, but not painful, just noticeable or maybe even a bit uncomfortably hot, but still painless enough that you can stand in them.

7. Keep growing the flames as you inhale but now imagine the sphere turn from a deep black, to a pale black. It should be as if the flames are burning away the color from the sphere.

8. As you continue on the next inhale see the sphere turn a light grey color.

9. Finally inhale again and see the sphere turn completely white.

10. Now that you are standing on a white sphere, see the flames gradually go out. Relieve yourself from the feeling of the flames and just see the ball of white light.

11. Inhale again and see the white sphere grow as bright as you possibly can.

12. Now begin to visualize a tube of white light going from the top of your head all the way to the center of the Earth. Think of it like a straw, but of white light.

13. Visualize the Earth beneath you as a sphere of bright green light. At this point you'll be standing atop a white sphere, that sits a top a huge green sphere, with a tube of white light through your body connecting it all.

14. Inhale white light from the universe and see it flow through the tube. Watch it rush from the top of your head to the center of your body and fill out your body with white light.

15. Now when you exhale, visualize the tube of light that's in the center of the Earth. While exhaling see the green sphere glow and begin forcefully drawing a black smoke out of the energy inside your body, and put it through the tube. See the black smoke travel and be absorbed by the green sphere of energy. It will completely cleanse and dissolve in the energy of the Earth while removing it from your body.

16. Repeat steps 14 and 15 over and over again until there is no more black smoke or at least a very feint black smoke leaving your body. The white light represents you drawing in divine energy, while the Earth pulls the negative energy from you represented by the black smoke. Try to really feel any negative experiences leave your body as this happens. This can be anything from physical pain, anxiety, or just general bad energy, but try

to feel it leave you as the Earth takes it in your visualization.

Once you have completed this exercise you will be grounded. You may even feel your feet still be slightly uncomfortable from the flames you visualized if you were able to fully immerse yourself. You have essentially burned out the bad energy and used the energy of Earth to cleanse it and purify it. This is another example of energy transfer. You didn't remove that negative energy from existence, but you transformed it through this formula into energy that is now within the Earth that can be repurposed. At the same time you filled yourself with purer, more divine energy to equally replace all the more negative energy that was once there. Ideally you will be full of divine energy at this point. A good thing to try directly after this would be the Qabalistic Cross again to seal in the energy and strengthen it further.

The Middle Pillar

The Middle Pillar is fundamental, and well practiced technique by many Ceremonial Magickians. This ritual is similar to the Grounding Meditation, and even provides the same benefits. The primary purpose of this ritual is much different than simple grounding however. The purpose of the Middle Pillar is to both connect ourselves to "the source" and ground us in our true will. This exercise has us proclaim outwardly that we are one with "the source". It reminds the universe around us, as well as our own internal workings that we are "the source", and we are connected to it, so our will is to be executed.

1. The Middle Pillar is also ideally performed while standing, but modify it as needed for your physical abilities.
2. Close your eyes and relax your body.
3. Inhale and visualize a bright white light enveloping everything above you. This represents "the source" as a pool of divine energy.
4. Above your head visualize a bright, white sphere. Inhale 4 times, each time see the divine light above you pour into this white sphere. Fill the sphere and see it glow as brightly as possible.
5. Focus on the white sphere above your head. Inhale 5 more times, but now when you exhale vibrate *Eheieh* (Eh-he-ay) each time. This is a divine name of God and means *"I am"*.
6. Let the energy flow from your head to your throat. Visualize a grey sphere in your throat. Just like before inhale 4 times and see the sphere glow as bright as possible.
7. Now focus on the grey sphere in your throat, inhale 5 times just like before, but this time when you exhale vibrate *YHVH Elohim* (Yay-ho-wah El-oh-heem). This is another divine name of God that means *"The Lord God"*.
8. Move the energy to your chest and visualize a gold sphere. Inhale 4 times and see the sphere glow as bright as possible each time.
9. Focus on the gold sphere in your chest and inhale 5 times. Each time you exhale vibrate *YHVH Eloah Va Da'ath*

(Yay-ho-wah El-oh-ah Vah Dah-ath). This divine name or phrase means *"of knowledge and wisdom"*.

10. Visualize a sphere just above your pelvis that is purple in color. Inhale 4 times again and see the purple sphere glow as brightly as possible.

11. Focus on the purple sphere and inhale 5 times. This time as you exhale each time vibrate *Shaddai El Chai* (Sha-dye El-kai). This divine name means *"The Almighty"*.

12. Move on to your feet and see the energy flow into a black sphere that is enveloping your feet. Just like in the Grounding Meditation see the sphere in the ground, but instead of standing atop it, have it cover your feet. Inhale 4 times and see it glow as brightly as possible.

13. Focusing now on the black sphere, inhale 5 times and on each exhale vibrate *ADNI Ha Aretz* (Add-on-eye Ha Ah-rets). This divine name means *"Lord of the Earth"*.

14. Visualize a green sphere beneath you that is the size of the Earth. Like before this sphere represents the energy of the Earth and nature. Inhale 4 times and see it glow as brightly as possible each time.

15. Take a moment to focus above yourself, visualizing "the source" that you drew all this energy from. Once focused, inhale deeply. As you exhale see white light flow through your body and connect each sphere all the way from "the source" to the Earth. This step connects it all together and increases the energy you've conjured up. It is actually a non-traditional step and is optional if you wish to stop at step 14. Incorporating this last step simply amplifies all the work done and provides a clean wrap up, but it's not needed.

16. Clap, snap, or stomp your foot to return from your focused state as you open your eyes again.

Mastering The Middle Pillar is going to be one of the most beneficial things you can do before moving on. Doing so will constantly cleanse, charge, and grow your energy. You are quite literally connecting yourself to the purest form of divinity each time, and growing yourself closer and closer to it as you do. Do this as often as possible as you start your practice. As you go forward, continue to incorporate it as often as you see fit. There are other rituals which satisfy the same goal as The Middle Pillar, but The Middle Pillar is fundamental for a reason. It is worth emphasizing to yourself that all the rituals you learn in this text will be footholds that you can always return to. Often Ceremonial Magickians benefit greatly from returning to basics, especially after diluting themselves with complex practices over time.

These rituals are fundamental not because they are "basic", but because they are the most powerful by far. Ceremonial Magick is interesting this way as you learn some of the most powerful techniques first, and then focus them in toward specific goals later as you grow. As you will learn later, regular banishing and cleansing is important to continue growth and not dilute your practice. Some of these foundational rituals may not be very targeted or powerful for a specific intention or goal, but you may try to direct the energy in anyway you see fit. That said, other rituals exist that help target specific goals, but if you need a clean slate as you practice, foundational rituals like The Middle Pillar are immensely powerful solutions. If you ever feel overwhelmed come back to The Middle Pillar to center yourself. This is a powerful technique for any practitioner of Ceremonial Magick no matter how advanced.

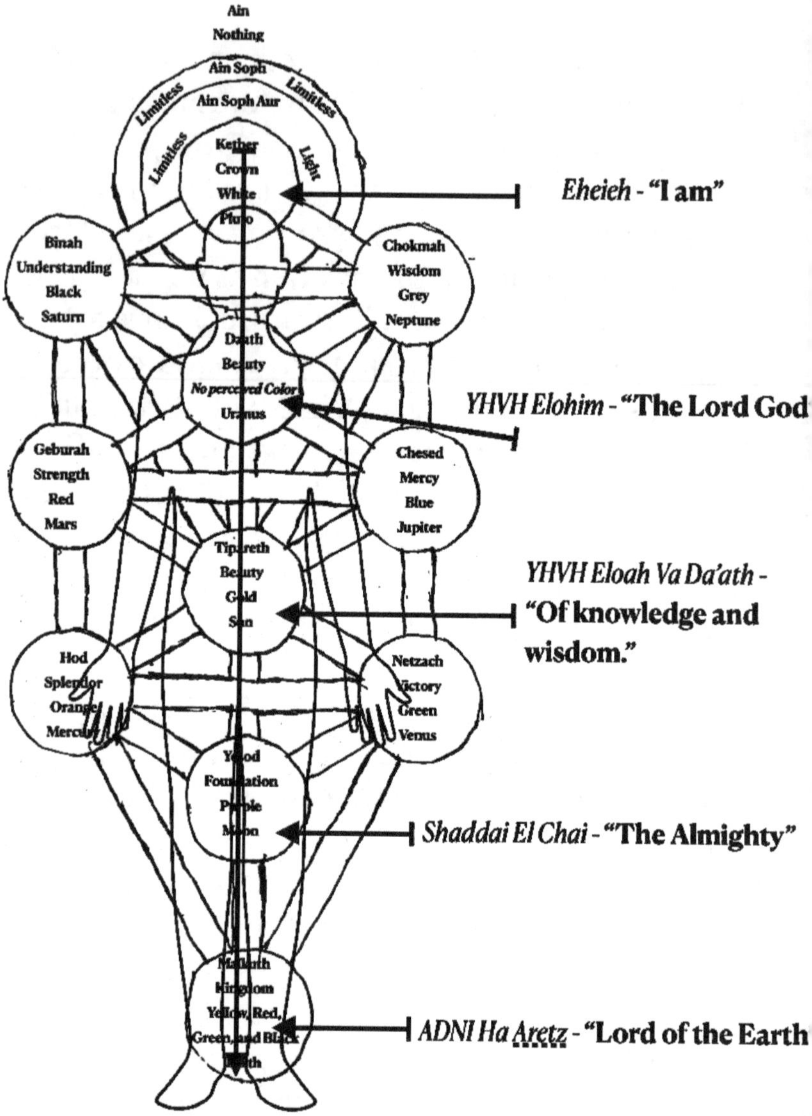

The Middle Pillar - Technical Representation with the Tree of Life

Chapter 7: Cleansing Rituals

Hopefully by now you have a good grasp on the concept of energy in general. Understanding that energy never really leaves, but transforms is powerful knowledge. With this we can also begin to understand why cleansing energy is necessary. This is because energy lingers. If you don't put in the effort to transform energy into something else, the natural energy around will begin to pile up. Add that to anything you bring to the table as you go about life and you can end up with an energetic mess.

How does one go about cleaning an energetic mess? Well there are quite a few ways. The Middle Pillar is one for purifying and cleansing yourself, but sometimes you may need to clear a space. There are not only techniques founded by Ceremonial Magick to accomplish this, but also some pretty useful Natural Magick tools that will help you do so a little more passively (or in tandem to enhance a Ceremonial Magick technique).

Natural Cleansing

Natural Magick provides insight to material, sensory, and the physical practices to perform cleansing of a space. Many people who practice some form of Natural Magick like to use things like herbs or incense to clear a space. Some common tools would be items like:

+ White Sage
    + Cleansing, healing, protection, wisdom, manifestation.
+ Lavender
    + Cleansing, sleep, love, happiness, relaxation, healing.
+ Frankincense
    + Cleansing, astral travel, courage, purification, consecration, protection, meditation, luck.

White sage is a typical go to and is revered as a default spiritual cleanser. You may have even seen it in movies that have some spiritual component. It has become so engrained into pop culture that most spiritual practitioners are aware of its properties before they even dive in. This is one thing that is actually mostly correct in terms of esotericism in pop culture. However, as effective as white sage is, it is not the only cleansing herb. Often I use frankincense instead since it is a bit easier to find in your general off the shelf shops, and is equally as powerful.

It is also important to note that white sage has drummed up some cultural drama in recent years. While the founding of this discourse is extremely murky and interesting, the social impacts of said discourse are not a focus of this text. What is a matter of fact however, is since white sage has become "trendy" in present times, it is in high demand. This has led to some problems in acquiring white sage ethically, and has even led some dishonest vendors to sell fake white sage. This is only worth noting as a precaution to a beginner at the time of this text's publication. Growing your own can absolve any supply or ethics issue, but most beginners are likely not growing their own herbs. It is very common for practitioners of any status to not undertake such a task since it can be a cumbersome practice on its own entirely. Make sure with any herbs, incense, or essential oils that you are purchasing or growing a legitimately trust worthy product.

Keep in mind lavender, frankincense, and other more available herbs are just as effective for cleansing, so don't get too hung up on using one over the other. It is recommended to start with the ones listed in this text, but feel free to research correspondences with other natural tools and add them to your practice. To cleanse a space with these tools, simply light some incense in a room, diffuse an essential oil, or use a smudge stick and manually go through your space. Opening all doors and allowing the air to flow will enhance this cleansing further, but natural airflow in most modern spaces will carry the energy as well.

In addition to this you are going to want to physically clean your space. Dirt in a space is not only not ideal to live with, but it is a physical representation of residual energy that you don't want impacting your work. Simply sweeping will actually prove extremely effective at cleaning a space. Be sure to dust, sweep, and generally clean your space until it is noticeably clean. It doesn't need to be spotless, so don't over do it, but definitely physically clean in addition to burning different herbs and oils. Not only will these activities cleanse a space spiritually for your practice, but they also literally keep the space clean. Magick really is one to one with impacting the physical world and vice versa. This is where you may see the phrase "as above, so below" appear. Things we do on a spiritual level impact the physical world, and things we do on a physical level impact the spiritual worlds. Natural Magick cleansing practices are an excellent medium to demonstrate this. As above, so below.

Sign of Silence

The Sign of Silence is an extremely powerful technique. In my opinion it is likely the most simple, yet powerful, for clearing a room. I always make the joke that if ever I had to perform an exorcism of some sort, and the Sign of Silence doesn't do the trick, then the problem is either not a spiritual issue, or there is something really wrong occurring in the universe. You may have already partially done this technique if you chose to stomp your foot at the end of a meditation or ritual in early practices of this text. There are just two additions to complete it. To perform the Sign of Silence do as follows:

1. Place your index finger over your lips like you're about to tell someone to shush.
2. Visualize a bright white light above you. This is the divine light from "the source" again. Let it encompass everything above you.
3. Stomp your foot, don't do it too light or too hard, just with intention and purpose. As your foot hits the ground visualize the white light come down and clear the entire space.

From here on out it is recommended to conclude all ritual work with the Sign of Silence. This is a traditional way to conclude Ceremonial Magick work and is extremely effective at leaving a place cleaner than you found it. The sole purpose for this technique is simple, powerful, and effective at spiritually cleansing a space. It's even discrete enough to use publicly whenever you enter a new space. While ideally done standing, it can be done in any position that allows you to stomp your foot. As you gain more experience over time, this is one technique that you may eventually be able to reproduce with no physical action. Simply walking into a room, then visualizing and feeling the energy take action for cleansing would be a great goal to reach. However, perfecting rituals isn't the point of Ceremonial Magick, achieving TGW is, so don't get too caught up on power when it comes to rituals. It benefits you none to be a powerful ritual worker if you can't use those rituals to complete TGW.

The Lesser Banishing Ritual of the Pentagram

The full Lesser Banishing Ritual of the Pentagram (LBRP) will be detailed in two chapters later on from this section. It is discussed here as it is important to preface the purpose of this ritual first before diving in. The LBRP is by far the most important ritual you will learn in practicing Ceremonial Magick. Traditions like the Hermetic Order of the Golden Dawn would have initiates master this first before inducting them into higher orders. While it is no longer necessary to follow such a strict system to grow our individual practices, it is important to realize they were structured that way for a reason. Understanding that reason allows us to grow at our own pace without moving too quickly to things that may leave us confused. The LBRP is used before almost every single ritual that you will learn going forward. Even if it is not expressly required, this is at minimum a ritual that should be practiced daily. Whether you do a more advanced form of the LBRP, or just the basic, it will consistently cleanse your space while simultaneously drawing you closer to achieving TGW.

Some people may be a little hesitant when they see the word "pentagram". While the symbol has gained some negative reputation over time, it is important to realize a pentagram is merely a 5 pointed star. It is a symbol that was long used by many cultures, even by Christians, before it was adopted to be purposefully blasphemous by those that wished to spite other faiths. There is nothing evil about it, in fact it used to be used to represent each of Jesus's wounds when he died on the cross (10). It is even true that groups like Satanists don't use this to do any evil. Just because a certain religion is feared or revered by one practice or the other does not make one "good" or "bad". The morality is extremely subjective based on your perspective. A Satanist performing the LBRP can achieve the exact same "good" thing that a Christian could. Using these examples hopefully demonstrates and resolves a classic western point of friction in religion and spirituality. Keep in mind other paths like Wicca and Norse Paganism were also persecuted in similar ways by other religions. The implication that society puts on a symbol is just that, an implication, what matters is how it is used.

In Ceremonial Magick the pentagram has a very specific meaning and use. More so this symbol even dates back to ancient Sumerian pottery and was often used as a symbol for deities like Ishtar (10). The pentagram is just a bit of symbolism, but don't be mistaken, it is powerful symbolism. No matter how you put it, symbolism is extremely important in Ceremonial Magick. Symbols are precisely why we use visualization in rituals. Symbolism communicates to our subconscious better than words at times. Ceremonial Magick practitioners have simply done the work to determine which symbols are best for which use case in a given ritual over time. The pentagram is one that corresponds with divinity and the natural elements. Each point represents something different. The top point represents spirit or divinity, the right point represents water, the left point air, the bottom right fire, and the bottom left earth.

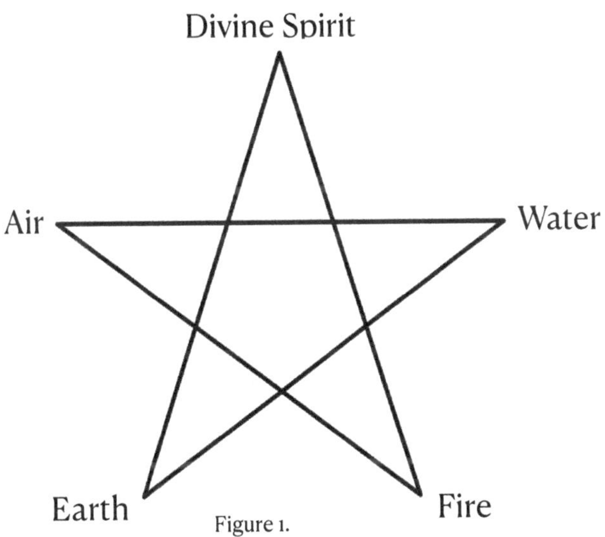

Figure 1.

The symbolism within the LBRP also further corresponds to various angels that are in charge of these elemental correspondences. When you do the LBRP you are balancing all the elements to master them, and what they can do for you on a spiritual level. When doing the LBRP you first begin with grounding yourself spiritually via the Qabalistic Cross. Once grounded, you will be evoking four angels around you that cleanse and protect the space you are working in. You then direct these angels to carry out your will. At first this will be done by working with their most common correspondences. From there, once you understand how the ritual works, you may use it to accomplish specific goals based on your own will. Once you finish, you close out once more with the Qabalistic Cross to seal in all the energy you created in the cleansed state, then administer the Sign of Silence to clear the room. As you might be able to tell, we are going to begin incorporating the building blocks of what you've practiced thus far. If you are still not quite comfortable with a given technique, continue to practice it. Don't jump into the LBRP until you feel ready. At the same time, it is okay to jump in and not do so perfectly. If you end up making a few mistakes the first time around just make sure you take notes on what to fix, and try it again once you're ready. Try not to take things too seriously, this practice is a serious practice, but you only see the benefits in success. If you beat yourself up over mistakes all the time you will hinder your progress, not help it. Take it seriously in the moment and when it works, but not after the fact. Magick will continue to work whether you know it is or not. Let it work, and focus on your growth.

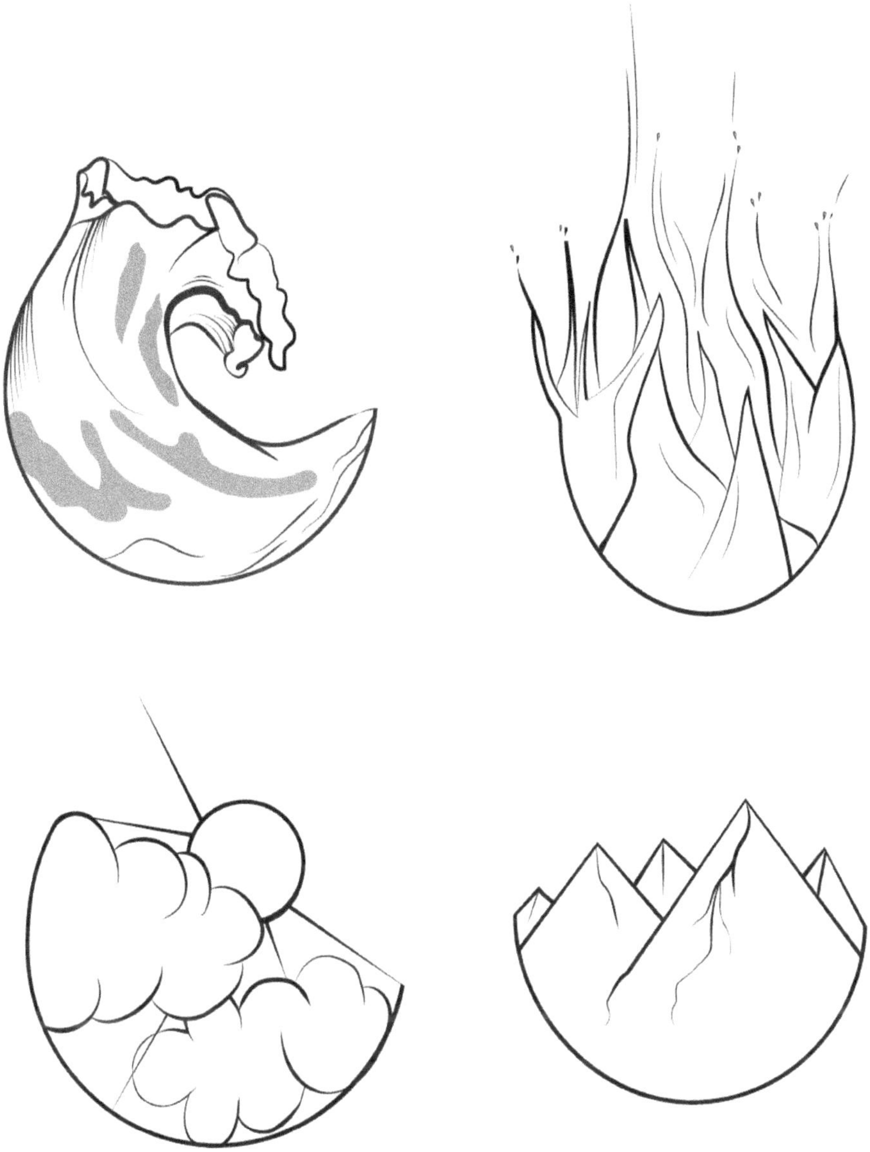

The Four Elements - Artistic Representation by Mikayla Thompson

Chapter 8: The Magickian's Circle

The Magickian's Circle is an exercise I didn't find until well into my practice. This is a ritual that seems to have its roots in the basic idea of "casting a circle". The purpose of casting a circle is to create a sacred space for ritual work to be conducted within it. In Ceremonial Magick this is precisely what the LBRP is for, however the LBRP is not the only way to go about casting a circle. Many traditions that practice some form of magick teach their students how to cast a circle. I first learned of this ritual from Jason Louv, in his YouTube video *"Enter the Magician's Circle"*. In this video Jason uses this exercise in the form of a guided meditation to introduce people to the concept of Ceremonial Magick. Since then, I've worked with this exercise over time to see what all benefits it could provide outside of meditation.

What I learned by focusing on this in a more ritualistic context is that it can be used for many things. It is amazing for grounding first and foremost. During the ritual you'll draw in massive amounts of energy. No other beginner ritual I had conducted prior ever required drawing in as much energy as this exercise at the base level. Due to the mass amounts of energy you'll be pulling in you essentially saturate the space around you and ground yourself in the light of divinity.

In addition to grounding you also go about casting a very large circle of flaming blue light. This allows you to consecrate the space in which you cast the circle, therefore making it a space in which ritual work can be conducted. It is not a replacement for the LBRP as you will see going forward. The LBRP requires working with greater and more focused energies and achieving a certain balance. If you just need a neutral space to conduct your work in however, The Magickian's Circle is excellent.

Self Initiation

In Ceremonial Magick traditions, especially notable orders such as the Hermetic Order of the Golden Dawn and even the Ordo Templi Orientis, there were ranks. If you were able to successfully join an order, you had to be initiated. Initiates were required to master certain rituals before being allowed to learn secrets of the higher ranks. Some of these orders still exist to this day in their own lodges. If this is of interest to you simply research what sort of Ceremonial Magick orders have lodges near you. Be sure to research them heavily before joining though. While this is good general advice for joining any group, it is critically important to analyze what a given order is teaching. If their teachings don't quite align with what you learn from reading on your own, there could be something off.

Since many of their rituals became public it is very easy to research what you should expect. Books like this, *"High Magick"* by Damien Echols, and even going to the source material like the *"Original Account of the Teachings, Rites, and Ceremonies of the Hermetic Order"* republished by John Michael Greer, would be of exceptional benefit for your reference. More so you can easily search the internet for many free resources and information on these same rituals, ideas, and philosophies. Check if they line up with a given order you'd be interested in joining. There are many benefits to joining an order if you can, but be aware that once you do so, you'll be learning from a teacher that will guide you along a specific path. A good teacher will help you carve your own path from there. If you're the kind of individual that thrives with a formal teacher, formally initiating with an established order might be a good idea.

That said, initiation is done simply by doing the work. Even if you join a group, your initiation work won't be much different in scope and focus than if you had done it on your own. It can feel a little confusing to learn all this new information and suddenly start calling yourself a Ceremonial Magickian, but I assure you, once you begin the work, you are exactly that. Even still, some may desire a formal milestone to demonstrate their progress.

At this point you should have meditated endlessly, learned to cleanse, and even performed traditional ritual work at the most basic level. To solidify your transition and begin putting these building blocks together, perform The Magickian's Circle, and consider it to be your initiation ritual. Once you have mastered this ritual, not only will you have grown yourself immensely, but you will be more than prepared to take the next step.

In Tarot, which is taught in later sections, you may think that "The Magician" card is representative of a Ceremonial Magickian's status and initiation. However, while "The

Magician" is a very important card that has a correspondence of strengthening magickal ability, it is not representative of the journey that you are undertaking. Rather it is a tool to represent continuation and growth as you go. All Ceremonial Magickians start as, and forever remain, "The Fool".

You may think "The Fool" is insulting at first glance, but "The Fool" is arguably the most powerful card in the Tarot. This card represents a banishment of all anxiety and worry. Being carefree and moving forward, as a "fool" who is unaware of the dangers ahead. More importantly it is also representative of undertaking a new journey. That is precisely what we are doing as Ceremonial Magickians. We are throwing caution to the wind, ignoring what we were told, and trying to carve our own path. By initiating yourself, you join the ranks of us fools, and may proudly call yourself a Ceremonial Magickian. Continue your growth, but never stop being a fool in this sense. Embark on your journey and execute your true will.

The Magickian's Circle

This ritual serves the purpose of centering yourself in your true will. The visualizations require you to constantly push beyond the boundaries of what you think you are capable of. Each time you do this as you grow, you will be asking more of yourself, and each time you should try to push beyond the limits of what you think you can do. Eventually you will experience that there is no limit. That what you can achieve is infinite. This ritual helps you experience that sensation while simultaneously grounding you, and creating a sacred space where you may perform other works. To conduct The Magickian's Circle, observe the following steps:

1. You can perform this standing, sitting, or laying down. Be sure you are comfortable and in a place you can focus. Close your eyes once you are in place.
2. Start with the Four Fold Breath. Do this between 2 to 4 times, whatever works best for you.
3. Once your breathing is stable, imagine a circle drawn around you in blue flame. Make the circle as big as the room you are in.
4. While you visualize this circle think of this specific intent: "In this space there are unlimited possibilities".
5. Now think about a time that you felt at your absolute best. Think of this memory, try to relive it. Breathe the air you breathed at that point in time, feel the sensations you felt, and really try to experience the memory again as if it is happening right now.
6. Let that memory fade gradually. Now begin to remember a special time in your life. Something that seemed impossible and magical to you. Experience that memory again the same way.
7. As that memory gradually fades, begin to recall a time when something that you wanted to achieve just happened. This can be anything, big or small, but once again try to fully experience and relive this memory.
8. Look to your body and try to feel the energy within you as you exist currently.

9.   Try to move the energy around your body, circulate it. Move it backwards and forwards. Try moving it to different sections of your body. Feel it exist as physically as you can within you.

10. Try to grow the energy, see it get brighter.

11. Identify if there are any colors associated with the energy and make them brighter.

12. Double the energy you've observed. See it grow brighter.

13. Double the energy again, do this over and over. Each time you think it can't get any brighter, challenge yourself and double it again. The energy will start to become so large it expands beyond your body. Keep growing it.

14. Continue growing the energy until you form a sphere of it within and around the circle. It should completely envelope you. Double it once again even at this stage.

15. Begin to think about who you are. Think about what you want to achieve.

16. Think of the 3 goals outlined below. As you think of them, visualize yourself as if you have already achieved them. Experience how that feels for you, and imagine what others would say. Try to really experience your joy and success as if it has already happened. As you think of each of these goals double the energy again each time:

     1.   Something that you want to accomplish today.

     2.   Something that you want to accomplish this month.

     3.   Something that you want to accomplish this year.

17. Once you have completed visualizing your accomplishments, double the energy once again, even if you think you can't.

18. Open your eyes, and gradually come out of the meditative state.

19. Get up and continue your day. Don't focus on the work of the ritual you just did. Move onto the next ritual if you are doing one, or simply carry on as normal. This is important because you've already manifested your intentions. If you over focus on them you hold onto them and the energy you've given them. Release them and let them come to pass. You have already achieved them, the future will always eventually become the present.

Congratulations, welcome to the path of Ceremonial Magick. I'd argue that you were already on it since you began reading, but with this you can truly cement that notion within yourself. From here on you will be controlling the universe by controlling yourself and vice versa. As above, so below.

The Fool - Artistic Representation by Abbie La-Fey

Chapter 9: The Lesser Banishing Ritual of the Pentagram

As taught in Chapter 7, the Lesser Banishing Ritual of the Pentagram (LBRP), is a powerful cleansing ritual. In this chapter not only are steps to conduct the ritual documented, but also a more refined explanation is provided in the context of what you are actually doing with it. The purpose of the LBRP is to create a clean, protected working space for all other ritual work. It is commonly used by Ceremonial Magickians to conduct the LBRP both before and after any other ritual work. Doing so before hand prepares the space, and doing so afterward clears all excess energy and seals the energy you generated in your aura to carry out your intent.

When you conduct this ritual you are evoking 4 archangels that represent the 4 elements of Air, Fire, Water, and Earth in an attempt to balance and direct their energies. This means you are calling external energies from the universe to carry out a specific intention. It can be anything from using known correspondences to create general life improvement, all the way to using the ritual to contribute towards the completion of you true will. This text will provide verbiage to always be doing both, but feel free to add or remove what applies to your specific goals.

As implied by the word "banishing" you might think to your self, "why are we evoking and bringing in external energy?". As alluded to in previous chapters, in Ceremonial Magick we do not make use of our own energy, rather the energy of the universe around us. This is what gives us infinite possibilities in what Ceremonial Magick can achieve. So yes, you actually are bringing in outside energy to your space, but this is energy you are bringing in intentionally. If you really wish to completely cleanse a space that is what the other cleansing techniques such as Natural Cleansing and the Sign of Silence are for. However, the LBRP allows you to both totally cleanse a space, and replace it with specific energy to carry out a task that you assign.

With this exercise you will need to be familiar with a few new concepts in Ceremonial Magick. The first is the "sword mudra". In Ceremonial Magick traditionally the LBRP is conducted using a a myriad of tools. The instructions provided by the Golden Dawn require you to have tools such as:

+ An altar
+ Physical objects representing the four elements
+ A ceremonial robe
+ A sword

While these things are useful to have, they are by no means necessary to conduct this ritual. The "sword mudra" is the only new thing that will need to be understood. It is a very simple hand gesture that replaces the sword used by the traditional ritual. Simply choose the dominant hand you wish to use for the ritual and form a fist with your middle and index finger extended on your hand. An image of how it should look is provided here:

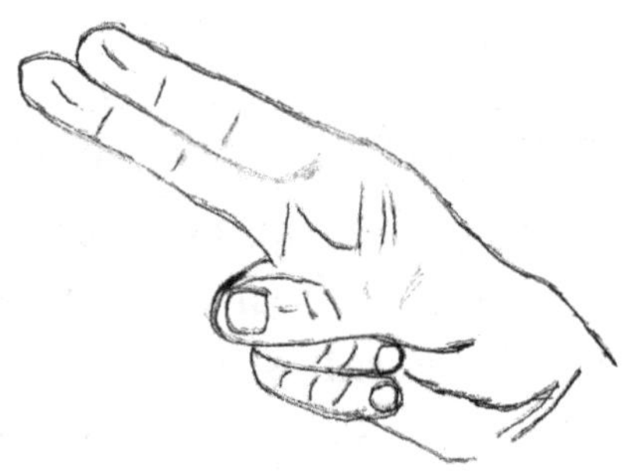

Figure 2. Sword Mudra

The other thing you will need to know going into the ritual is how to draw the pentagrams around your space. For the LBRP pentagrams are drawn from the bottom left corner up. You can use your body as a reference for how big to make them. The bottom left corner should start at your left hip, connect to the top of your head, then your right hip, followed by the left shoulder, then with the right shoulder, and ending back at your right hip. A diagram for directional purposes is provided below:

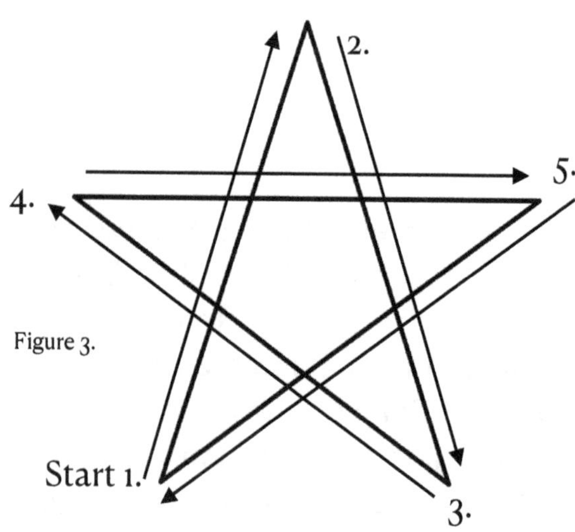

Finally, you need to understand a few new "mantras". These are the various names of "God", or the "Divine", and names of the angels you will be vibrating through the ritual. The names of the Divine are as follows:

+ *YHVH* (**Yehowah**) - God.
+ *ADNI* (**Adonai**) - Lord.
+ *AHIH* (**Eheieh**) - I am.
+ *AGLA* (**Agalah**) - The source of all creation.

The names of the archangels you will need to know are as follows:

+ **Raphael** - *The healing of God*, archangel of *air*. Represents ideas of safety, healing, assistance with meditation, focus, and intelligence.
+ **Gabriel** - *The strength of God*, archangel of *water*. Represents ideas of overcoming emotional pain, healing, and love.
+ **Michael** - *There is none like God* or *The Power of God*, archangel of *fire*. Represents ideas of protection, strength, and passion.
+ **Uriel** - *Light of God*, archangel of *earth*. Represents ideas of divination, wealth, and material goods.

You may notice that each of these angel names end in *"el"*. While not every angel name does, often archangel names do, and when they do it's no coincidence. These two letters in Hebrew are often translated to *"of God"*. In Ceremonial Magick this is significant for correspondence purposes. Angels are not deities or even really their own entities. They are intelligences and representations, but they do as commanded by the universe in the natural transfer of energy. Angels are intelligences that are used by Divinity, hence why they are referred to as "of God". Because these concepts are their own intelligences, they are not God, but rather a stepping stone to allow us to achieve certain goals as if we were God. With the LBRP these angels can help us achieve goals related to the correspondences of the four elements we recognize in nature.

By calling down divinity, these intelligences desire to help us and draw us in closer, it is their natural function. We can use rituals like the LBRP as a formula to direct that function in our own lives. When you evoke all these angels around you, you will then give them instruction. This will change their core function as it relates to your will in the universe. Anyone is capable of this, but without the formulas we call ritual, no one would really know how. The LBRP is the first milestone that really binds the basic concepts together to help you achieve a new kind of complete work in Ceremonial Magick.

Even if you don't believe in angels, remember, these are symbolic representations of actual physical sources of energy that we have mapped to correspondences of real physical properties. Naturally as you change them in your life, then the universe will respond accordingly. That said, it is important you revere and respect this energy, it is not yours, and you are controlling it. Treat your focus and intentions to focus on your will and you will naturally see it occur. This is the way these intelligences work. Why they do so is something we aren't exactly sure of, but it is observable by nature and in practice. At times not knowing the intricacies of why something works is frustrating. It is not very insightful outside of the results, and that is often why many rituals can be viewed as hypothesis.

Acknowledging that shortfall is important, because it means there is simply more that we do not understand. Sometimes we actually do come to understand these things with continued ritual work, and that is how intricate correspondence diagrams and definitions come to be created in time. Otherwise it is up to the individual practitioner to determine the deeper roots based on their own experience. The good news about Ceremonial Magick is that there is no faith required in this mystery. While we may not have all the answers, or even all the formulas, we do have many of them. Even if a formula doesn't have a deeper meaning, what is beautiful is that if it works, it works. The deeper meaning ultimately doesn't matter as long as it helps you achieve TGW. That doesn't mean throw caution to the wind and never dig deeper, but sometimes we don't have the time to and need results. That is where not needing faith or blind trust makes Ceremonial Magick tangible. It will either work or it won't regardless of why.

Think of this like someone who uses a computer every day. Many people sort of know how they work. They know there's some mechanical parts that do some complex actions, and eventually there's software that makes interfaces they can interact with, but that's about it for most people. Even an experienced professional in Computer Science can't often tell you the precise programming of every logic board and computer chip for every system. That is important to observe, because some people do fully understand those mechanisms because these machines are finitely complex. The universe on the other hand is infinitely complex, so it only makes sense that we know even less about the inner workings currently. The lesson here is that just like a user doesn't need to know the inner workings of a computer to browse the internet or write a book, even the most skilled Ceremonial Magickian doesn't need to know every detail that composes the universe. It is how you shape your will and your place in the universe that matters.

Since this text is focused on the basics of actually doing the work that is Ceremonial Magick, we will not dive too deeply into why some things work the way they do unless necessary. The LBRP is actually a very refined ritual with its roots deeply sunk into the broader correspondences represented by concepts like the "Tree of Life" and the "Shem HaMephorash". Teachers like Damien Echols have spoken to these high level concepts in very precise, easy to understand ways. Other than researching them yourself, I'd recommend looking to similar teachers to broaden your history in the roots of the LBRP. The focus of this text is simply to teach you what it is for and how to do it in modern practice.

LBRP

To perform the LBRP you will need to find a private room where you can be a lone and focus. While it is perfectly okay to have others present once you have mastered this ritual, it can be both awkward and distracting if you try to do it with others before learning it yourself. To conduct a traditional LBRP observe the following steps:

1. Center yourself in the room which you are conducting the ritual. You will have your eyes open at first.
2. Identify the cardinal directions of the space, and begin by facing *East*.
3. Conduct the Qabalistic Cross ritual. This will seal and cleanse your aura and provide protection within yourself. More importantly, this brings in the energy that we will used to conduct the ritual.
4. Begin to visualize a connection from the divine energy pulled in from the Qabalistic Cross and see it connect into the Earth. Visualize the Earth as a brightly glowing green sphere and the energy connecting the Divine, to you, and the Earth, as bright white light.
5. Facing *East*, form your hand to match the sword mudra and raise your arm directly in front of you. Walk forward if you would like. You are about to cast a circle so you may make it as big or as small as you want. Be sure you clearly define the boundaries though so you consecrate the exact space you intend to for your work.
6. Inhale white light from above, and visualize this energy flow down your arm that is forming the sword mudra. You are going to visualize directing this energy into reality before you.
7. Draw your first banishing pentagram directly in front of you. Visualize it being drawn in blue flame coming from the light of your fingers in the sword mudra.

8.   Inhale white light again and thrust your fingers through the center of the pentagram and see it burn even brighter.

9.   Vibrate the mantra *"YHVH"* (Yeh-ho-wah). As you do so see the pentagram glow infinitely brighter.

10. Lightly tap your foot to represent sealing the energy of this pentagram.

11.   Inhale again and use the sword mudra to begin drawing a line of bright white light from the center of the *Eastern* pentagram. Walk to the *Southern* wall of your space drawing the circle of light util you are directly facing it.

12.   Inhale white light again, and draw your next pentagram the exact same way to the *South*. This time vibrate the mantra *"ADNI"* (Ad-oh-nai). Make the pentagram glow brighter as you do so just like before.

13.   Once again, inhale and pour energy into the center of the pentagram and see it glow even brighter.

14.   Lightly tap your foot to represent sealing the energy of this pentagram.

15.   Inhale and draw the white line now from the *Southern* wall to the *Western* wall until you are directly facing it.

16. Draw your next pentagram using the mantra *"AHIH"* (Eh-he-ay) and see it glow brighter.

17.   Charge the center of the pentagram the same way as the others.

18.   Lightly tap your foot to represent sealing the energy of this pentagram.

19. Inhale and draw a white line from the *Western* wall to the *Northern* wall.

20. Draw the final pentagram and vibrate the mantra *"AGLA"* (Ah-gay-lah) and see it glow even brighter.

21. Charge the center of this pentagram the same way you did the others.

22. Lightly tap your foot to represent sealing the energy of this pentagram.

23. Inhale and draw a white line from the *Northern* wall back to the center of the pentagram on the *Eastern* wall.

24. Now return to the center of your space within the circle of pentagrams if you have not already.

25. Facing *East*, extend your arms out to each side of you so you are standing in the shape of a cross.

26. Say the words *"before me"* then vibrate the name *"Raphael"* and try to visualize an angel before you in bright yellow robes. Raphael is associated with having a caduceus so if it helps, integrate that into the visualization. If you find it difficult to visualize your own representation of an angel, just start with a simple ball of bright yellow light. This will work just as well.

27. Now say *"behind me"* and vibrate *"Gabriel"* visualizing an angel in bright blue robes with a silver chalice, or simply a bright ball of blue light.

28. Next say *"on my right hand"* and vibrate *"Michael"* visualizing an angel in bright red robes with a sword, or simply a bright ball of red light.

29. Then say *"on my left hand"* and vibrate *"Uriel"* visualizing an angel in bright green robes with a pentacle, or simply a bright ball of green light.

30. Take a moment and visualize the space with all the angels and pentagrams around you glowing infinitely brighter.

31. Now state aloud, *"for around me flame the pentagrams"*.

32. Inhale, close your eyes, and visualize a hexagram in the center of your chest. See the upper triangle that

forms the hexagram flaming in brilliant red, and the lower triangle in a flaming blue.

33. Open your eyes again. Say aloud, *"and within me shines the six pointed star"*.

34. Now inhale, and bring your arms up until your palms touch above your head. Visualize that you are shaping the top half of a sphere of white light that encompasses the space.

35. Extend your arms back to their original position and inhale again. Begin to bring them down and close the bottom half of the sphere of light beneath your feet. Remember focus on the visualization, even if the movements aren't quite right that is more than okay, everyone can do it a bit differently. Be sure your intentions and visualizations are your primary focus as that is the core of the work.

36. At this point you may now conduct any ritual that you wish to within this space. Try performing the Middle Pillar in this space now and draw in even more energy. This is also a good time to issue a command to the angels around you. Keep in mind there are other rituals purpose built for invoking and directing angels, but the reality is the angels are now in this space with you. By acknowledging this, you may instruct them on what to do with the energy that brought them to surround you. Often issuing a task to each based on correspondence is beneficial. You could ask Raphael to increase your wisdom, Michael to protect you fully, Gabriel to provide healing, and Uriel to increase your wealth. Be sure to issue a task to all 4 elements, it is not required, but you'll want to do so to balance the elements in this base version of the LBRP.

37. To conclude the ritual conduct the Qabalistic Cross again to seal all the work you've done in your aura.

38. Once complete open your eyes from the Qabalistic Cross and see the visualization of the LBRP fade gradually. Don't force it out, but see it naturally fade if you can. This will help smooth the transition between states of consciousness and energy exchange.

39. Conduct the Sign of Silence to fully clear the rest of the space. Do this only after your visualization has faded.

Congratulations, this is a huge milestone! You have completed the LBRP. This is a ritual you will want to conduct daily at minimum, and definitely before any rituals you do going forward if you can. It's actually perfectly fine to conduct rituals without cleansing, but cleansing first with the LBRP, or even using the LBRP to issue intent helps you to be sure you only work with the energies you intended to work with, and not any excess energies created by you or anything else in the universe.

After completion of this ritual the angels you worked with will remain with you to be called on throughout your day. As you practice more these angels will actually start to be with you indefinitely since you will be constantly filled with divine light. Try not to focus too hard on the intentions or goals of the rituals you conducted after the LBRP, let them go. As stated before, if you focus on the energy you're holding it back and giving it more energy that it likely doesn't need. Simply acknowledge that your work is done, and live as if it is going to be fulfilled. Let the thought go and live life as you would normally.

EHIH - *Gabriel* - West - Water

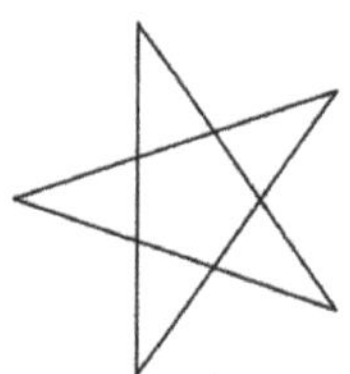

ADNI - *Michael* - South - Fire

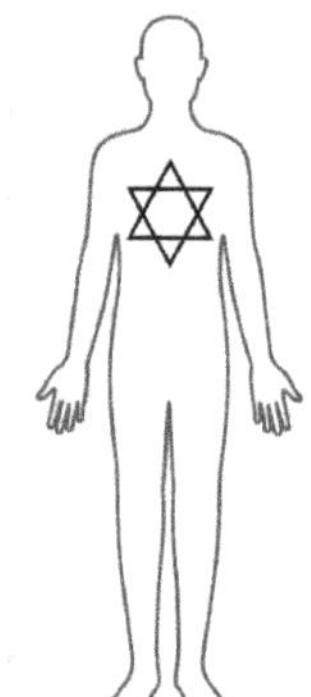

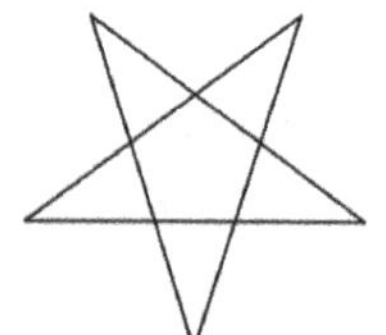

YHVH - *Raphael* - East - Air

AGLA - *Uriel* - North - Ea[r]

Lesser Banishing Ritual of The Pentagram Layout

LBRP Modifications

From here as you study you will be able to practice modifying the LBRP formula. One basic thing you can start to do is only working with one archangel at a time. To do this you simply replace all the names of Divinity and the angel correspondences to be repeated for the sole intelligence you desire to work with. For example if you want to work with Michael for immense power and protection instead of evoking all four you would simply vibrate *"ADNI"* for all four pentagrams, and vibrate *"Michael"* to be before you, behind you, on your right, and on your left, visualizing only Michael. From here you could issue a task to provide protection and strengthen you.

Another modification taught by Damien Echols, that has shown to be effective to some practitioners is to add two more angels. One will be above you, and one below you. Damien teaches a use of the angels *Metatron* and *Sandalphon*. By placing Metatron above you and Sandalphon below you, the space is fully guarded by angels from every angle. That said, this is a practice specific to Damien, but as you may be able to determine, by closing the space in a sphere of white light, you are fundamentally already doing this. However, it never hurts to draw in more energy. If you wish, you could replace Metatron and Sandalphon with two more evocations of Michael for more energy towards protection and power like in the example above.

Damien's use of other angels in the LBRP is completely valid and extremely creative in terms of modifying the LBRP formula. You see, as long as you use the right correspondences and divine names that would fit into the formula, you can modify it to get very different results. Damien teaches on this extensively in his work *"Angels and Archangels"* which is strongly recommended as a follow up reading for students of this text who may be interested in more rituals like this one. Working with angels related to Abrahamic faiths is not the whole of Ceremonial Magick, but in the early stages it is the primary focus. You will eventually move on to other works, with other energy sources, and intelligences to complete TGW. Knowing that, it is still true that Ceremonial Magickians usually start here for a reason.

One idea is that by working so much with the source and divine this way, and using angels to fulfill our will, we are building the "armor of god". This is talked about in The Bible, in Ephesians 6:10-18. In Ceremonial Magick however, this is interpreted as bringing as much of divinity to you as you can before moving on to new sources of energy. You are trying to saturate yourself in divinity so that way the universe responds to you as if you are something of importance. This is because you are, you just haven't reached your full potential in the present moment yet. Starting here grants you power and access to all other spheres of divinity in a logical and straightforward manner. Mind you, no matter where you start in terms of traditions, you will always work with "the source" so if you adapt a different entry structure to start with, or come from one already, that is still valid.

The simple fact is even though many Ceremonial Magickians may start here, eventually they will need to dive into other practices corresponding to other traditions and faiths. This lets them work with many other powerful deities and intelligences that are part of this collective consciousness observed across generations. Not every Ceremonial Magickian will need to know and practice everything in every area of theology, meta-physics, and meditation. What you do need to access and how much of it will be determined by your own path. Be sure to follow your path and observe your true will in action through it.

In conclusion for the LBRP overall, be sure to practice this daily. This can be your primary ritual for a very long time if you choose to make it so. This ritual alone will provide immense growth and focus for you practically and spiritually just by saturating yourself in divinity and balancing the natural elements. Once you feel like you've comfortably mastered it, you'll still continue to use it in your practice in some form, so go ahead and continue forward. Memorizing and understanding this ritual will prove immensely useful as it is once again, a building block for more complex rituals that you'll learn as you go.

Caliel	*Leviah*	*Hakamiah*	*Hariel*	*Mebahel*	*Ielael*	*Hahaiah*	*Lauviah*	*Aladiah*	*Haziel*	*Cahethel*	*Akhaiah*	*Lelahel*	*Mahasiah*	*Elemiah*	*Sitael*	*Ieliel*	*Veliah*
Menadel	*Chavakiah*	*Lehahiah*	*Iehuiah*	*Vasariah*	*Lecabel*	*Omael*	*Reiiel*	*Seehiah*	*Ierathel*	*Haaiah*	*Nithhaiah*	*Hahuiah*	*Melahel*	*Ieiaiel*	*Nelchael*	*Pahaliah*	*Leuviah*
Nithael	*Nanael*	*Imamiah*	*Hahaziah*	*Daniel*	*Vehuel*	*Mihael*	*Asaliah*	*Ariel*	*Sealiah*	*Ielahiah*	*Vevaliah*	*Mikael*	*Hahahel*	*Ihiaziel*	*Rehael*	*Haamiah*	*Aniel*
Mevamiah	*Haiaiel*	*Iabamiah*	*Habuhiah*	*Rochel*	*Eiiael*	*Menakel*	*Damabiah*	*Moehael*	*Anauel*	*Iahhel*	*Umabel*	*Mizrael*	*Harahel*	*Ieilael*	*Nemamiah*	*Poiel*	*Mebahiah*

72 Archangels of the Shem HaMephorash - Francis Barrett (1801, The Magus)

122

Chapter 10: The Analysis of the Keyword

The Analysis of the Keyword is another simple, yet extremely powerful ritual. It is far less complex than the LBRP, however it's often wise to do along side the LBRP once you have concluded it before you finish with the Qabalistic Cross. What is The Analysis of the Keyword, and more importantly what is "the key word"? This ritual can also be known as the *LVX* ritual. This is because *LVX* in Latin is *"light"*, and "light" is the keyword. The phonetic pronunciation for this word would be *"lux or lukes"*. In this ritual you will form each Latin letter with your body as you call divine light into your space. It might feel like a silly dance you may be familiar with, but I'll let you ponder that, remember don't take things too seriously!

LUX

To perform The Analysis of the Keyword ritual ideally you will have just conducted the LBRP and are intending to strengthen it. That said, even without the LBRP you may perform LUX to call down a huge burst of divine energy that can be channeled into anything you'd like. You can use it to enhance a ritual like the LBRP, charge a sigil, or even cleanse a space.

1. Center yourself in the room which you are conducting the ritual. If you just did the LBRP stand in the same center space you did when concluding facing *East*.

2. Close your eyes and bring your attention directly above you and try to visualize the universe above you.

3. Begin to visualize the divine light above you like you do during the Qabalistic Cross. Just a brilliant, infinitely massive pool of white light.

4. As you focus begin to take slow and deep breaths and see the light glow brighter each time you inhale.

5. Raise your right arm until it is pointed vertically above your head, and your left arm straight out to the side horizontally. You should be forming the letter "L" with your body.

6. Say "El" out loud and see the light glow even brighter.

7. Now raise both arms above your head at a slight angle so they are forming the letter "V".

8. Say "Vee" out loud and once again see the light above glow brighter and brighter.

9. Lay your arms across your chest in the shape of "X".

10. Say "Ex" and see the light glow blindingly bright, as bright as you can make it.

11. Using a commanding voice state, "Let the divine light descend". Visualize the white light come down from "the

source" and fill up the room. Let it totally fill the area as brightly as you can see it.

12. Hold this visualization in your focus, as you do vibrate the mantra *IAO* (ee-ah-oh). *IAO* is another name for YHVH or "God". As you vibrate this mantra, see the light around you glow infinitely brighter.

13. Conclude with the Qabalistic Cross, the Sign of Silence, or move onto your next ritual if still working within your LBRP space.

That is the Analysis of the Keyword. This ritual directly connects you "the source" to pull down massive amount of pure, divine, energy. While it is simple, the representations are fairly clear even without heavily detailed knowledge. LVX is light, which represents the divine light, while IAO is a name of God that is used as a mantra in Kabbalah in reference to the Tetragrammaton. Most new to Ceremonial Magick may not have heard of Kabbalah or the Tetragrammaton before so consider that a good bit of history to study. Much of the rituals that come from the Abrahamic religions are based on those concepts. At minimum these correspondences are based in this practices, so we have a consistent reference path for rituals based in this tradition. As a result this whole ritual simply puts immense and immediate focus on divine energy directly from "the source".

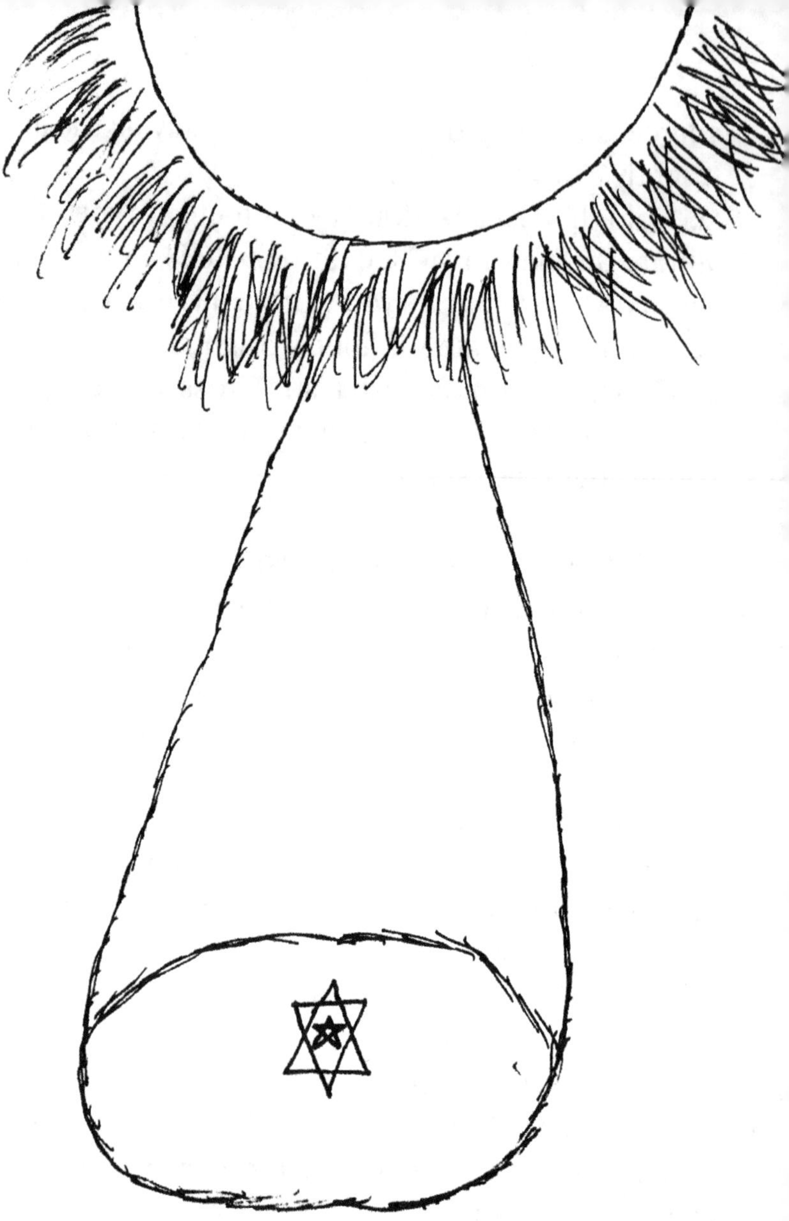

Divine Light - Artistic Representation

Chapter 11: Lesser Invoking Ritual of the Pentagram

The Lesser Invoking Ritual of the Pentagram (LIRP) is a ritual that is just like the LBRP with two distinct differences. The first difference you will notice is the direction in which you will draw the pentagram. As shown in the figure provided next, the starting point for drawing the pentagrams in this ritual is at the top of the star rather than the bottom left. The other difference is in the name of the ritual. You will be "invoking" energy this time instead of "evoking" and banishing. In the LBRP you evoke angels around you, and banish all other energy. The angels you evoked can still be given tasks, but it is mostly used cleanse the space and issue specific intents for how to do so. So while you can instruct the energy to carry out your will in the LBRP, that is not exactly what it is for.

The LIRP on the other hand is constructed exactly for the purpose of instructing and creating. The LIRP invokes the angels into and around you. This brings them into your energy and connects you to them for the purposes of instructing them. Once you do the LBRP, the energy around you will recognize you as a source of divinity, and as such, be ready to carry out any task you set out for them. Because of this, the LIRP is often carried out directly after doing the LBRP. The LBRP cleanses the space, and the LIRP is used to invoke and task the angels with your intentions.

The ritual is exactly the same as the LBRP in practice other than those two changes. One thing to note is there is no need to conclude the LBRP with the Qabalistic Cross or begin the LIRP with it. If you do both rituals back to back one Qabalistic Cross step at the very beginning, and one at the very end to conclude is more than enough. That said, feel free to execute it fully and perform the Qabalistic Cross in-between as often as you'd like. It will only improve your aura, but it is not needed for the ritual to be effective.

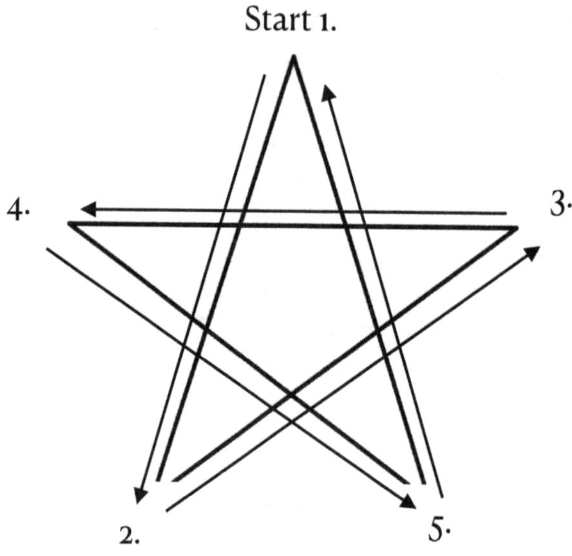

Figure 4.

LIRP

To perform the LIRP observe the following steps. By now the LBRP should be familiar to you so this ritual should be a bit easier to grasp. These steps assume you have completed the LBRP first, if you haven't be sure to insert the Qabalistic Cross prior to step 3.

1.   Center yourself in the room which you are conducting the ritual. You will have your eyes open at first.

2.   Identify the cardinal directions of the space, and begin by facing *East*.

3.   Facing *East*, form your hand to match the sword mudra and raise your arm directly in front of you. Walk forward if you would like. You are about to cast a circle again, so you may make it as big or as small as you want. Be sure you clearly define the boundaries so you consecrate the exact space you intend to for your work.

4.   Inhale white light from above, and visualize this energy flow down your arm that is forming the sword mudra. You are going to visualize directing this energy into reality before you.

5.   Draw your first invoking pentagram directly in front of you. Visualize it being drawn in blue flame coming from the light of your fingers in the sword mudra.

6.   Inhale white light again and thrust your fingers through the center of the pentagram and see it burn even brighter.

7.   Vibrate the mantra *"YHVH"* (Yeh-ho-wah). As you do so see the pentagram glow infinitely brighter.

8.   Lightly tap your foot to represent sealing the energy of this pentagram.

9.   Inhale again and use the sword mudra to begin drawing a line of bright white light from the center of the *Eastern* pentagram. Walk to the *Southern* wall of your space drawing the circle of light util you are directly facing it.

10. Inhale white light again, and draw your next pentagram the exact same way to the *South*. This time vibrate the mantra *"ADNI"* (Ad-oh-nai). Glow the pentagram brighter as you do so just like before.

11.   Once again, inhale and pour energy into the center of the pentagram and see it glow brighter.

12.   Lightly tap your foot to represent sealing the energy of this pentagram.

13.   Inhale and draw the white line now from the *Southern* wall to the *Western* wall until you are directly facing it.

14. Draw your next pentagram using the mantra *"AHIH"* (Eh-he-ay) and see it glow brighter.

15. Charge the center of the pentagram the same way as the others.

16. Lightly tap your foot to represent sealing the energy of this pentagram.

17.   Inhale and draw a white line from the *Western* wall to the *Northern* wall.

18. Draw the final pentagram and vibrate the mantra *"AGLA"* (Ah-gay-lah) and see it glow even brighter.

19. Charge the center of this pentagram the same way you did the others.

20. Lightly tap your foot to represent sealing the energy of this pentagram.

21. Inhale and draw a white line from the *Northern* wall back to the center of the pentagram on the *Eastern* wall.

22. Now return to the center of your space within the circle of pentagrams if you have not already.

23. Facing *East*, extend your arms out to each side of you so you are standing in the shape of a cross.

24. Say the words *"before me"* then vibrate the name *"Raphael"* and try to visualize an angel before you in bright yellow robes. Raphael is associated with having a caduceus so if it helps, integrate that into the visualization like before. Remember, if you still find it difficult to visualize your own representation of an angel, just start with a simple ball of bright yellow light. This will work just as well.

25. Now say *"behind me"* and vibrate *"Gabriel"* visualizing an angel in bright blue robes with a silver chalice, or simply a bright ball of blue light.

26. Next say *"on my right hand"* and vibrate *"Michael"* visualizing an angel in bright red robes with a sword, or simply a bright ball of red light.

27. Then say *"on my left hand"* and vibrate *"Uriel"* visualizing an angel in bright green robes with a pentacle, or simply a bright ball of green light.

28. Take a moment and visualize the space with all the angels and pentagrams around you glowing infinitely brighter.

29. Now state aloud, *"for around me flame the pentagrams"*.

30. Inhale, close your eyes, and visualize a hexagram in the center of your chest. See the upper triangle that forms the hexagram flaming in brilliant red, and the lower triangle in a flaming blue.

31. Open your eyes again. Say aloud, *"and within me shines the six pointed star"*.

32. Now inhale, and bring your arms up until your palms touch above your head. Visualize that you are shaping the top half of a sphere of white light encompassing the space.

33. Extend your arms back to their original position and inhale again. Begin to bring them down and close the bottom half of the sphere of light beneath your feet. Remember focus on the visualization, even if the movements aren't quite right that's more than okay, everyone can do it a bit differently. Be sure your intentions and visualizations are your primary focus as that is the core of the work.

34. At this point you may state specific intentions of any sort to any or all of the angels you've invoked. To start with something simple, try saying the following out loud: *"Raphael grant me wisdom and knowledge in Ceremonial Magick, Gabriel bring me healing, Michael increase my strength and provide protection in all things, and Uriel increase my abilities in divination and bring me wealth. Let all of this help me to achieve the knowledge and conversation of my Holy Guardian Angel within this lifetime, and achieve The Great Work within this lifetime. Let this bring about good to all and cause harm to no one. Let all of this come about in ways that bring about only blessings and never reverse, or bring about any curse, amen."* Do note, it is not necessary to speak aloud, but the more direct you are with anything you wish to manifest, the easier it is to feel it beginning to occur. This particular prayer simply addresses a few of the specialities of each archangel, and balances all four elements. It is good to begin with

if you don't know what direction to follow in your own mind. Feel free to say or think of absolutely anything you want in place of this when you are ready.

35. To conclude the ritual conduct the Qabalistic Cross again to seal all the work you've done in your aura.

36. Once complete open your eyes from the Qabalistic Cross and see the visualization of the LIRP fade gradually. Don't force it out, but see it naturally fade if you can. This will help smooth the transition between states of consciousness and energy exchange.

37. Conduct the Sign of Silence to fully clear the rest of the space. Do this only after your visualization has faded.

One more note on the sample prayer. You may notice that it is very specific and intentional about how you wish to achieve your goal. In magick of all kinds you will want to be extremely specific with your intentions. The reason for this is because these entities and energies you are now working with are going to do exactly what you say by any means necessary. Say you wanted to quickly earn lots of money. Well for all you know the quickest and easiest opportunity for the universe to give you that financial relief might result in physical harm. As an example, one way it may manifest is by you taking on a physical injury in which you can collect an insurance payment, but now you have a broken leg. Take that concept an apply an infinite array of possibilities and you never know what might happen.

With this in mind you will want to put parameters around your intentions. You can still be very high level in your instructions. For example, maybe it really doesn't matter to you how money ends up coming your way, but you at least know you don't want to cause an internal moral, or ethical, dilemma. In this case you should provide your intention with the parameters that the work should not be done in a way that compromises whatever integrity you have in your own heart. The words for this will need to be your own, but that is exactly the point in cases where you are defining the parameters. Be specific and intentional. The sample prayer contains an ending instruction that is a very minor variant of one method to end a prayer taught by Damien Echols. Overall the prayer encompasses the intention to provide you with knowledge, healing, power, protection, wealth, and growth. However it does so in such a way that keeps the focus on your true will, pulling you towards TGW, and obtaining the knowledge and conversation of the HGA. Further it states that all of this work, including pulling you to your true will, must be done in a way that only brings good and blessings to all and may never be reversed. This is a good generic ending to start with that lets the energy work to an infinite degree, but within the parameters of the universe that will be only of benefit to you. With that you can trust your work and move forward with confidence.

Now that you are capable of both banishing and invoking, you have all the baseline tools of a Ceremonial Magickian to carry out your will. There is still more to learn, but you may now begin a full and consistent practice. Build on what you have learned from here and continue to grow at your own pace. Congratulations once again!

The Magician Tarot - Artistic Representation by Mikayla Thompson

Chapter 12: Energy Work

Now that we've built a strong foundation of basics in Ceremonial Magick, it might be beneficial to get some more practical techniques into your tool belt. Not everyone in Ceremonial Magick focuses on energy work. Some people are more interested in subjects like divination, or sigil work. I tend to lean towards focusing on energy work because it is useful in doing everything in Ceremonial Magick, but it is not the only focus one may take on.

Since energy work is so versatile, it is often wise to at least teach the fundamentals. At the beginning of this text you performed some basic energy work already. This type of energy work was to give a practical foundation for what it feels like to even begin conceptualizing magick without all the rituals. From here that concept evolves into actually using energy from the universe around you and turning that into whatever you want. To begin you will learn to direct energy by noticing it in your body more acutely, and attempting to move it via visualizations.

Included in this section you will also learn a few more useful techniques for charging physical items, performing blessings, and creating thought forms. All of these techniques are useful in making the magick you are already doing more powerful. They will also give you the means to do magick every single day, even if you are unable to execute a normal ritual. Charging and blessings are techniques you can use every single day to fill an item with energy, or bless yourself or your meal to give your intentions even more strength.

Directing Energy

Directing energy is a technique that's easy to conceptualize, but very difficult to execute. When you generated energy via friction, you could easily feel the heat between your hands. What is neat about that exercise is that you can actually use it to begin practicing directing energy. It is a useful physical tool to help you feel what is going on outside of visualization. Your goal later on would be to direct energy without any physical assistance, but to start with assistance brings no harm at all. Try the following exercise to begin practicing directing energy with a specific intention.

1. Find somewhere to sit, stand, or lie down.
2. Perform the four fold breath until you are calm. Naturally close your eyes when you are ready to proceed.
3. Inhale and visualize a gold sphere in your chest, like you did for The Middle Pillar, and see it glow brighter.
4. As you exhale focus on the sphere and see it glowing brightly.
5. Repeat steps 3 and 4 over and over until you see the gold sphere glow as brightly as you can make it glow.

6. **Optional Physical Step:** Rub your hands together until the friction produces a noticeable amount of heat. Don't rub them so hard that it becomes uncomfortable, just enough to really notice that heat like before.

7. With your hands just slightly apart, visualize the energy from the center of your chest flow as a gold light down both arms, into your hands, and then begin to form a sphere of gold light between both hands.

8. See the sphere glow bright gold and try to feel the warmth it is producing between your hands.

9. Inhale and see the sphere in your chest glow brighter.

10. Exhale and direct the new energy into the sphere between your hands again.

11. Repeat steps 9 and 10 and grow the sphere between your hands as large and bright as you'd like. The more energy you put in, the more effective it will be.

12. Now think of an intention, maybe something you'd like to accomplish today. If you can't think of anything, just think about your desire to complete The Great Work. Put that intention into the sphere of energy that you're holding. Just focus on the idea as you see the light glow.

13. Now you're holding a sphere of really powerful light charged with an intention of your own will. You can visualize sending this light into anything you'd like. Since the other exercises will have better examples of this, for now simply hold the sphere of light to your forehead. Try and feel the heat of the energy against your forehead. See it glow as bright as you can.

14. Visualize the sphere of light enter your head. See it kind of phasing through you until it is within your body. See the light fill out your entire body and flow through

you. You will have just given yourself this energy containing a focused intention to complete a goal. This alone will make your actions extremely effective at carrying out whatever intention you put in. Imagine the possibilities that you could observe if you could put this energy into other things. You absolutely can! This is just the fundamental step.

Each step of the way, really try to focus on how the energy feels moving through your body. If you remember doing The Magickian's Circle, you might recall all the steps that were really encouraging your to think about and feel where the energy was in your body. You're doing the same thing here, but directing the energy externally as well. Once you feel comfortable, try omitting step 6 and see how strongly you can feel the heat by generating it from your mind via visualization, even without the physical sensation.

Charging

Charging something is the next natural step after learning how to direct energy. You can charge sigils, talismans, food, clothing, drinks, and even other people. Charging things is a simple and powerful way to store massive amount of energy for later use. Charging can be used to store energy in order to increase the power of more involved rituals later. It can also be used to simply allow for one to carry an item with them that is always doing magick, even when they may not be able to. To charge something stick with the same steps as in the "Directing Energy" section. This time instead of sending the energy into your self, pick an item. This can be a glass of water, a piece of jewelry, or even this book. Once you have your item, perform the Directing Energy Exercise, then observe the following steps once you reach step 12 in that section.

1.   With the item you wish to charge directly in front of you, visualize the sphere of energy going into it. Use your hands to push it into it. Touch the item if need be, but make sure you try to really feel and see the energy transfer occur from you to the object.

2.   Visualize the object glowing intensely bright with the energy. Really saturate every bit of it until all you see is the shape of the object, and the light from the energy.

3.   Open your eyes and feel free to use the object. Set it on a shelf, or altar space for safe keeping if you have one. Consume it if it was something like water or food, or wear it if it was jewelry.

You can also use this to provide healing to people or give them general energy of any sort. Be mindful that when working with other living things, especially humans, you cannot change some one else's will. That is not to say you can't try, it is just not ever going to be something you would likely want to do. You can change your own will, and the way the universe responds to you, because that is your decision and your control. As you've learned from the LIRP, even carving your own path can benefit from specificity in your intentions. Without such specificity, you may reach your goal, but at a cost you didn't foresee. Similarly, changing someone else's will requires their permission. Not having it can have unforeseen consequences. If you force it, technically it might work, but keep in mind the saying of "as above, so below". Even if you mean well, if it the action was not explicitly allowed by someone else, any negative outcome would reflect back on your own life doubly, and you would be the one that caused it. Especially if you elect to observe a malicious action on purpose, you are feeding the universe your own ill intent and telling it that is what you want for yourself as well. Point being, working with others will always backfire on you exponentially, *unless* you have their explicit permission. If you don't, you may still get exactly what you wanted to impact their life, but it will be at an incredible cost for you. Especially if you attempt something on a practitioner that is knowledgable in reversal magick. In that case, you will not only get a helping handful of the universe's reflection back, but also the full intent of your own work tossed right back to you, at no impact to your target.

In this manner there is no such thing as "evil" or "black" magick, at least not in the moral sense. The term "black magick" is technically synonymous with many other legitimate practices that are not malicious in nature. Rather, there is only magick for oneself, magick for the permitted benefit of others, and magick of malicious intent (even if you actually meant well, those backfiring energies still fall into that last category). It is common that new practitioners usually end up using magick for the manipulation of others will, be it on purpose or by mistake. It is a learning experience, and it is totally valid should you practice this way, but be cautious to not dig your own grave. Remember Ceremonial Magick is a practice of working towards enlightenment. You are not Merlin shooting fireballs, or the Wicked Witch of the West casting curses on your enemies. Those are fairy tales, this is a real practice with measurable results. With that of note, if someone gives you permission, you can absolutely direct energy with the intent to do something like heal, protect, or empower them. That is often very beneficial to those in need, or if you wish to do group work with other Ceremonial Magickians, witches, or the like!

Blessings

Now that you know how to properly direct energy, you can observe blessings. Blessings are extremely powerful, and are a quick form of magick that can be applied in even small moments of your life to make them even better. Two basic blessing rituals are walked through next. The first is just a basic blessing via the charging technique you've now hopefully mastered. The second is a full on ritual that can be used to bless yourself and others.

Blessing

This technique takes a component from the LIRP and the basic charging technique to create a quick, but powerful transfer of blessed energy to another object. In the steps below water is used, but you may replace water with quite literally anything you wish to bless.

1. Pour a glass of water and place it in front of you.
2. Close your eyes and use the Four Fold Breath to focus. Each time you inhale see bright white light above

you glow and begin to enter your body through your nose and mouth.

3. Once your body is saturated in white light, draw a small invoking pentagram above the glass of water using the sword mudra (the LIRP version drawn from the top of the star first).

4. Thrust your fingers through the center of the pentagram as you would in the LIRP.

5. Vibrate the mantra *"Yeshua"* (yesh-uah) and see the white light flow down your arm that is forming the sword mudra and saturate the glass of water. Yeshua is one translation in Hebrew for "Jesus". In Ceremonial Magick invoking "Yeshua" is representative of invoking what is known as "Christ Consciousness". Christ Consciousness varies slightly in meaning across practices, but one thing that is universally agreed on is that this concept is seen as a bridge between us and the divine. Invoking Christ Consciousness is akin to bypassing the "veil" for a moment as your own higher self, and using that to pull energy from "the source" very quickly.

6. See and feel the energy leave your hand and completely encase the glass of water in bright white light. As you do think of an intention, you may speak it aloud if you wish. This may be beneficial if you are doing a more formal blessing in front of others. For water you can bless it for something like good health, or even just let the blessing be the natural divine light. When you consume it, the work you've already put into the world will be able to use that energy to be more effective.

7. Simply say *"amen"*, or close the blessing however you wish, and open your eyes. Congratulations, if you used water you have now made a very potent holy water!

The concept of "Christ Consciousness" may be off putting to those who don't identify with Abrahamic traditions even more so than the idea of angels. What is important to note is this concept has always existed across ancient traditions as the idea of a "higher self". Essentially this is the you that has "pierced the veil". This you exists, you are just not experiencing it yet, you are building it. By invoking it, you can transcend for a moment to tap into the divine directly and quickly. Christian traditions invoke Christ Consciousness all the time and often refer to this as "being saved". One common teaching they also observe is to end prayers with "in the name of Jesus Christ, amen" or some variant thereof.

This is all just one way to go about invoking Christ Consciousness, but it is not inherently a Christian idea. Ceremonial Magick, as well as other traditions, essentially teach the same thing about Christ Consciousness that Christianity does, just taking it a step further. These traditions pick up where Jesus left off by teaching how to actually use this idea of a higher self. If nothing else, Christ might be seen as one of the greatest Ceremonial Magickians of all time. Something that other Ceremonial Magickians have pieced together as a result of Christ's work, is a way to consistently unify the mechanism by which we can do blessings like this. Rather than trying to invoke our higher self at times when we may have trouble fathoming such a concept, we can instead invoke Christ, who has done the work and transcended energetically. This energy source has been poured into for centuries. As a result, much like with the angels, we can now use this entity and idea of Christ to tap into the divine energy directly.

This of course is very clearly not the only way to do this. You can just as effectively and easily direct energy from the middle pillar or the LIRP and bless things the same way. In fact, you can also bless things with specific intentions using specific angels and other deities. Say you want to bless something to increase protection, instead of *"Yeshua"* you could vibrate *"ADNI"* and ask Michael for a specific blessing. Using "Yeshua" is just an all encompassing generic, but there may be times where you are focusing on a specific entity. In those cases it would be beneficial to direct focus on a specific entity instead of "the source". This formula is probably one of the easiest to modify to your personal path and swap out any deity from any tradition. Have fun making things "holy", but keep in mind that your intention is important and you should be certain of it before you bless anything or anyone.

Blessing Ritual

This blessing is a more focused ritual. You will want to use this ritual to bless yourself, another person, or even a space. Performing a blessing ritual like this can also be done in preparation for other ritual work. One practice to observe would be to use this to bless yourself, and others, before performing group work. This will help make sure all are protected and cleansed prior to beginning. If enough people are present, be sure to exchange blessings to increase the benefit to yourself and others.

1. Start by inhaling and visualize the earth beneath you. See the earth below you fill with bright white light.
2. Draw a cross in white light using the sword mudra on your forehead (or someone else's). As you do so say,

"Blessed be your mind, so that it is open and receptive to truth".

3. See white light rush up from the earth beneath you, through your hand, and into the cross of light on the forehead.

4. Inhale again and draw a cross over your/their heart. As you do say, *"Blessed be your heart, so that is is open to the giving and receiving of love".*

5. See the light rush up again and charge the cross over the heart.

6. Inhale again and draw a cross over your/their hands and say, *"Blessed be your hands that they may be strong enough to do the work that will be required of them".*

7. See the light rush up again and charge the cross over the hands.

8. Inhale one last time and bless the feet just as you did the hands by drawing a cross and saying, *"Blessed be your feet, so that they may carry you to the completion of your journey".*

You now have the knowledge to incorporate blessings into both your regular ritual work and even day to day life. The basic blessing was taught to me as a practice similar to how some people are taught to pray over their food before each meal. Not only is this blessing akin to the practice and usage of blessing food, but it is encouraged to use it quite literally anywhere on anything you see fit. You could bless a pencil before a quiz, your phone before a job interview, or your instrument before playing a show. It is extremely quick and effective. The best part of the efficiency is that it allows for performing powerful magick every day, even if you can't do a ritual in the current moment.

The actual ritual is a bit more involved of course, but knowing how to perform it is very beneficial as you find yourself growing and branching out. Techniques for cleaning, banishing, and charging are the fundamentals every practitioner of Ceremonial Magick will use each and every day. Whether it's part of a small blessing, or a large ritual, the more control and intention you have over your energy work, the better.

Thought Forms

Thought forms are a focused outcome from a manifestation ritual. There are many ways to create thought forms, in fact you might already create them all the time on accident. Since you're doing magick all the time, whether you realize it or not, at some point something you think will consume you and become powerful enough to manifest a physical change in your life. Taking control of that is precisely what Ceremonial Magick allows us to do/ That way we are only manifesting that which helps us achieve TGW and fulfill our true will.

These steps will guide you to create a "thought form". Thought forms are a form of energy that we create via visualization. We place a specific intention into them, see them before us, and like a balloon, allow them to float off. The key to a successful thought form is to let it go. Totally forget about it once it's released. Letting the thought go allows it to carry out your intention. Hanging on to it means you're still thinking about it and giving it energy. Thinking about it will always pull the thoughts back to you, so letting go is critical to this technique working.

1. Sit and relax.
2. Conduct the Middle Pillar ritual while sitting.
3. Once you've visualized the shaft of light created during the Middle Pillar, turn your attention to the bright gold sphere in your chest. Focus on it.
4. Inhale green light up from Earth and pull down the white light from the Universe. Visualize both streams flowing into the gold sphere in your chest.
5. Inhale again and charge the gold sphere further with this light. Repeat this until you are satisfied with the energy you've accumulated. Once is enough, but you may charge the gold sphere as many times as you'd like.
6. Raise your hands in front of you as if you are going to clap, but leave a gap between them of about 1 foot.
7. Exhale and see the gold light from your chest travel through your arms to create a sphere between your hands as it leaves them.
8. As you exhale think of the intention you wish to manifest. Focus on it and feel the intention flow into the energy sphere that is in your hands.
9. Inhale and vibrate *"Yeshua"* (yesh-uah and see the sphere glow brighter.
10. Release the sphere and see it fly off until it is gone.
11. Forget about the sphere and the intention you set in it. Allow it to fulfill your will as you move on to whatever you'd like.
12. Clap your hands to conclude and regain present attention.

It cannot be emphasized enough that you must let go of the thought form completely. It might still work even if you bring it up to yourself from time to time, but it may take a bit longer. Consider every after thought once the primary thought is released to be like a chain. The chain yanks the energy back a little each time until it returns to you. As long as you aren't pulling the thought to you all the time, it will eventually complete the work, but the more effective you are at letting go, the quicker it will complete.

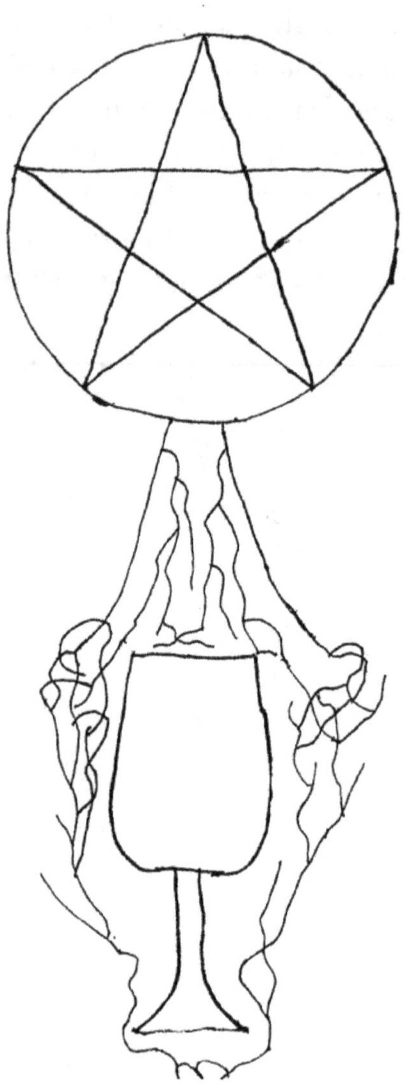

Invoking Pentagram Blessing - Artistic Representation

Chapter 13: Sigils and Talismans

Sigils and Talismans serve a very similar function in Ceremonial Magick. As you will see, it really doesn't matter which type of objects that you utilize, but incorporating one or both into your practice can be very beneficial. Based on Israel Regardies work, a "talisman is an object that has been magically endowed with the power of attracting good fortune." (7). Further Damien Echols expounds on Talismans and Sigils in his book "Angels and Archangels", using both types of objects for performing various sorts of angel focused Ceremonial Magick (6). What is a sigil and why is it different than a talisman and vice versa?

A Sigil is a specific series of patterns you create. Through the entire creation process you focus intent and energy into the creation of your Sigil. There are many methods to producing Sigils, but in this text you will be guided in how to create Sigils using the Rose Cross Sigil Creator. This is not the only method of creating Sigils, in fact you can apply what you learn directly to the Rune Sigil Creator that many Norse Pagan practices utilize. They all work very similarly, just be sure you understand why and how to create Sigils in general before you move to other formats.

A Talisman on the other hand can be literally anything. You could even repurpose a Sigil as a Talisman, however that is a bit redundant. Essentially a Talisman is anything that you bless with an energetic purpose that is not intentionally a Sigil. You could use a candle, a necklace, a piece of clothing, or even a paper weight. Similarly you can make Talismans out of anything, and if you do, just like you would focus intent in the creation process for a Sigil, you'd do the same for a Talisman.

The purpose for both of these items is exactly the same. They serve as a sort of energy storage container. You can use these items to store energy for a specific intent. You could imbue a Talisman with energy for protection and wear it. Each time you charge it during your ritual work it would become more effective and potent at carrying out that intention each time. Another example might be to charge a Sigil that represents an archangel, like Gabriel. You could store massive amounts of energy that corresponds to Gabriel into the Sigil over time. Once you are ready, you could burn it during a major ritual for Gabriel to enhance the ritual even further, without having to perform other works to gather energy. It gives you a way to do major energy work over a longer period of time, or create various tools for yourself to manifest certain goals and ideas.

When using these items for manifestation, especially Sigils, it is wise to observe the same practice you would when creating a Thought Form. Essentially once the Sigil is charged, forget about what you charged it for. Some people choose to bury it in the ground near their house, or in a safe space like a box in a room. Some keep it in their altar for safe keeping to protect it from other energies, and others simply leave it hanging as decoration or for other miscellaneous purposes. The idea here is to place the energy into the object, and let it work, just like you did the Thought Form.

While not necessary, it is recommended to incorporate both Sigils and Talismans into your practice. An easy way to begin doing so is to use Sigils as "active" working tools, and Talismans as "passive" working tools. What this means is a Sigil should be a focused piece that will carry out a specific purpose, either to store energy for a ritual later on, or to be used immediately by the creator for its purpose. The Talisman on the other hand would be used as something like a favorite necklace, ring, or accessory. You can charge this with anything you'd like and keep it on your person to fulfill its purpose passively as it should.

Keep in mind you don't have to stick to this use case, it is just a beginner methodology to help you start incorporating both types of tools. As soon as you feel comfortable creating and using both, it is strongly advised to experiment around with different intentions and purposes for these objects. The next two sections will outline some common methods of both charging, and releasing energy from Sigils and Talismans respectively.

Sigils

At the end of this chapter you'll learn how to create Sigils, but before you dive into that, let's make sure using them is clearly understood. Some common things to try when creating, charging, and releasing energy for a sigil are as follows.

Creating:

1.   Using a template or by hand, draw your sigil. As you draw it be constantly thinking of keywords and the intention that is going into the what the Sigil ultimately represents.

2.   Draw outer rings around the Sigil. In the rings use further keywords like the name of the archangel, or the word of the intention, and write these things in a circle around the Sigil. As you do focus energy into each letter for your desired intention.

Charging:

1.   Use simple energy direction techniques and charge the Sigil formally using the LIRP, Middle Pillar, or even just simple charging.

2.   Create a Thought Form and embed it into the Sigil for long term keeping instead of immediate release.

Releasing Energy:

1.   Burn the Sigil. This is the easiest and most straightforward way to destroy and release energy kept within a Sigil. Keep in mind, while it will destroy the Sigil, the energy is also released, so be mindful not to just burn random Sigils you didn't make.

2.   Bury the Sigil. Burying the Sigil imbues the earth around it with the same energy over time. Eventually natural transference of energy will drain the Sigil of its energy, but the execution of your intention will be carried out first.

3. Store the Sigil in the open. Similar to burying, leaving the Sigil in the open air will gradually release the energy into the space around it and ultimately to the universe.

Talismans

Since Talismans can be quite literally anything, there is really nothing to teach on the creation of Talismans. It is a valuable enhancement to be able to make your own Talismans, but it is not necessary at all. Simply choose any object you'd like to use, and make sure you only use it for that purpose to be most effective with your energy. The common ways to charge and release the energy however are exactly the same as with Sigils.

Charging:

1. Use simple energy direction techniques and charge the Talisman formally using the LIRP, Middle Pillar, or even just simple charging.
2. Create a Thought Form and embed it into the Talisman for long term keeping instead of immediate release.

Releasing Energy:

1. Burn the Sigil. This is the easiest and most straightforward way to destroy and release energy kept within a Talisman. Keep in mind, while it will destroy the Talisman, the energy is also released, so be mindful not to just burn random Talismans you didn't make.

2. Bury the Talisman. Burying the Talisman imbues the earth around it with the same energy over time. Eventually natural transference of energy will drain the Talisman of its energy, but the execution of your intention will be carried out first.

3. Store the Talisman in the open or wear it. Similar to burying, leaving the Talisman in the open air will gradually release the energy into the space around it and ultimately to the universe.

Creating Sigils

Creating Sigils is a very simple, but quite intimidating process if you've never done so. Fortunately, you can't actually mess it up. A Sigil could literally be a series of random lines, as long as you bring the intention, the symbolism won't be impacted. That said, using powerful, ritual focused symbolism can help your energy be more potent. This is the exact reason we use so much symbolism in Ceremonial Magick to begin with. Our conscious brain can speak to us with language, abstract ideas, and images, but our unconscious brain speaks with us almost entirely in visual images. Our dreams are visual communications sometimes. Our subconscious processing doesn't always just speak up with a direct thought, but rather through imagery like dreams. These visuals are how our brains try to process and communicate ideas in a subconscious state, such as sleeping.

What Ceremonial Magick does is use symbols like the Pentagram, the Hexagram, and various other visual elements to communicate more directly with our subconscious. Our conscious understands logically what these symbols mean, and what they map to. Our subconscious on the other hand can't internalize the words easily, but it can internalize the imagery. This is why Sigils are so effective, it is a way to create further visual stimuli to speak to, and direct our subconscious with. By following the standard practice, as opposed to drawing literally anything, you will be drawing symbolism that has purposeful and direct correspondences to the work you wish to achieve. That is not to say custom Sigils that use no framework are useless, it really is all about the intent, but you will miss out slightly on the established communication to your subconscious unless your symbolism also matches natural universal correspondences.

The Rose Cross Sigil Creator comes in two forms, English and Hebrew. The English version is the exact same as the Hebrew, just with a translation for the relevant English alphabet letters that correspond to the original Hebrew. You'll notice some letters are missing, this is because you will still need to spell the name or intention in the correct Hebrew linguistic context. Your Sigil can be anything, but commonly a good place to start is with an archangel since you can often find imagery of other Sigils for these same entities that you can compare your work to. This is just to help you make sure you are reading and using the Sigil creator correctly.

Once you feel confident you may use the Sigil creator to form any word you want, not just the name of an angel. The common way to spell out words is to omit repeating letters, and even vowels. You can choose to spell the whole name, word, or phrase out if you wish, but the longer the word, the more difficult it will be to compose a Sigil. The reason omitting letters is a common practice is simply because in the process of creating the Sigil, you'll draw a line back to the repeated letters, and depending on where the line comes from, it could result in not moving the line at all, or hitting a letter you've already marked. Essentially it's redundant in the Sigil drawing process, but that doesn't mean you have to do things that way if you prefer more direct specificity.

On the last page in this chapter there will be both English and Hebrew templates in full pages that you may use to trace for creating your own Sigils. Feel free to start out just using normal pencil and paper. Some recommended tools will be provided at the end of the chapter.

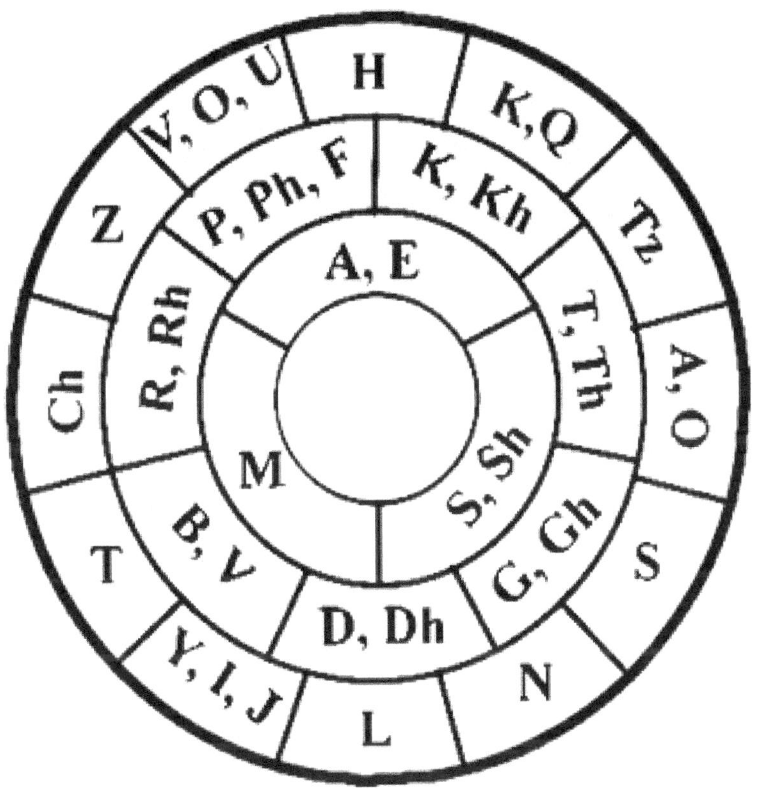

Figure 5.

1. Using the template, create a Sigil for the Archangel Michael.

2. Start by drawing a circle to mark the "M" in the Sigil creator. The circle should be an open circle, but for visibility it will be filled in through these steps. This is your starting point.

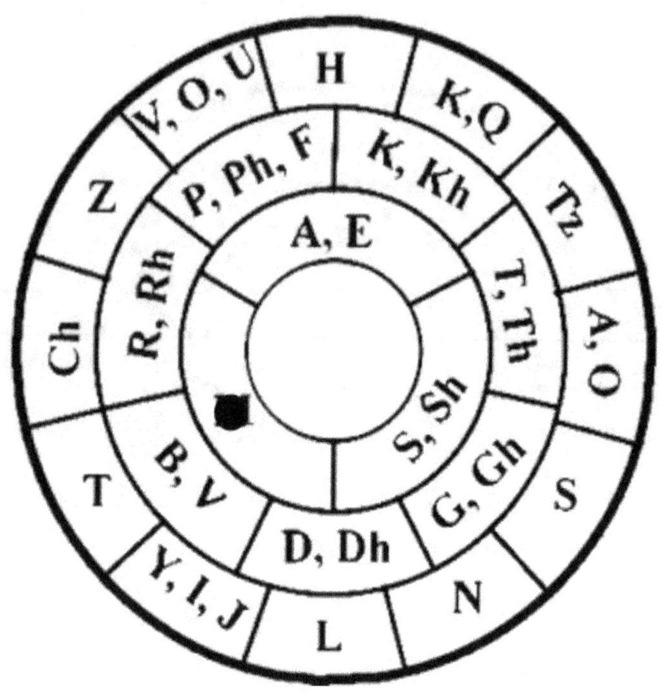

Figure 6.

3.   Next draw a line to the letter "I" in the "Y, I, J" space of the Sigil creator. Make sure it's a straight line directly to the next letter.

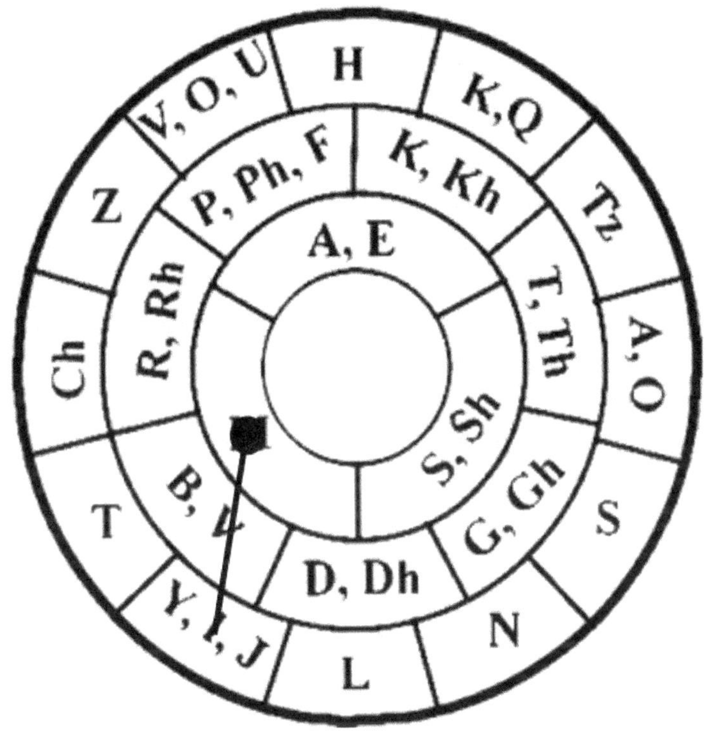

Figure 7.

4. Now we will draw a line to "K" or "Kh" space. This is because there is no Hebrew for the "ch" sound in the English spelling of Michael, but it does correctly correspond to Hebrew via this spelling.

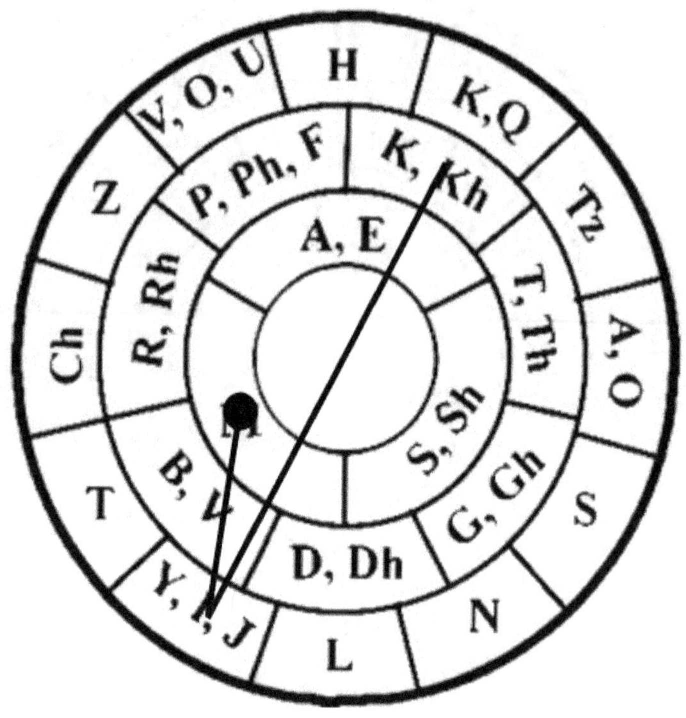

Figure 8.

5. Next draw a line going through the "A, E" space. The only necessary letter here is "E" to complete the "El" or "of God" ending in Michaels name. However, this space encompasses both letters we'd need for a more complete spelling, so both are addressed in either case.

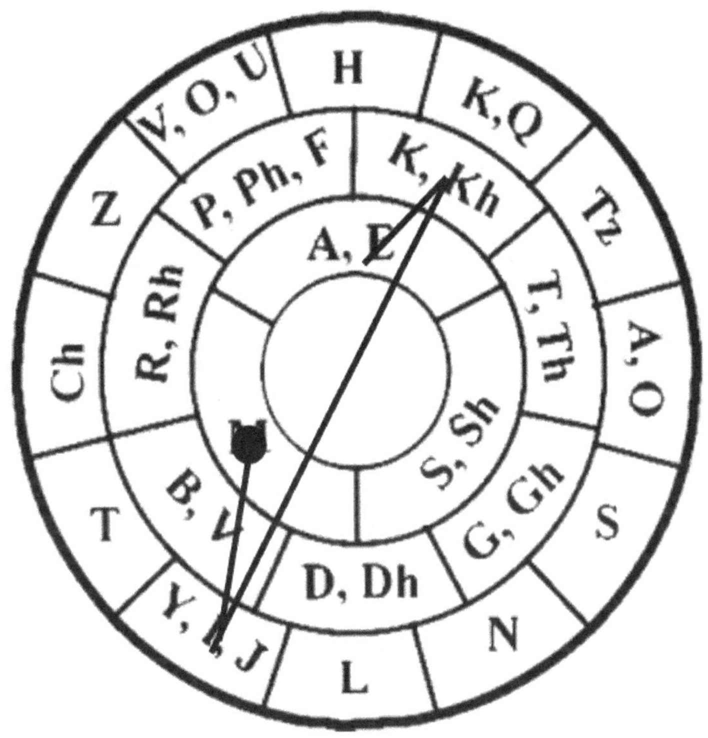

Figure 9.

6. Finally draw a line to the "L" space. Once you do so, end the line with a small horizontal mark to show this is the end of the Sigil.

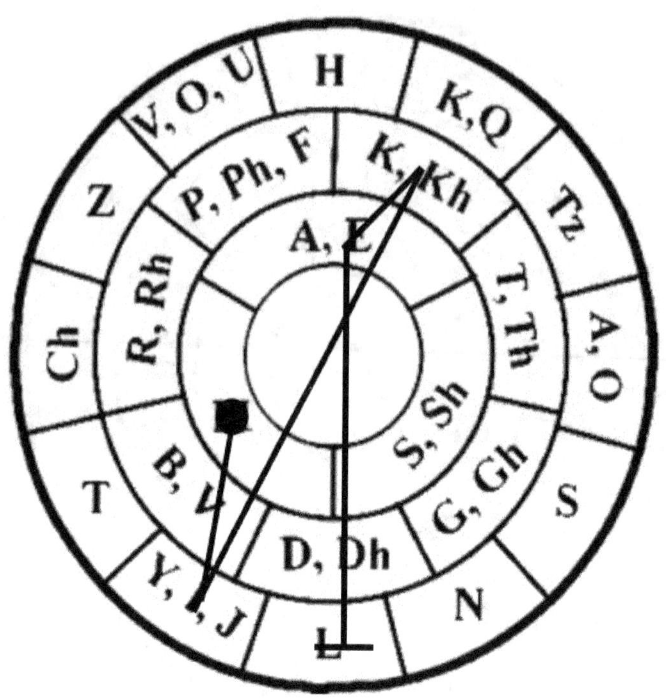

Figure 10.

7.   Congratulations you have now created a Sigil for the Archangel Michael! The final sigil removed from the template is shown below.

8.   Now that you are familiar with the creation process, focus on a specific intention, and go back and recreate the Sigil. As you draw, focus your energy and intention into each line. Once it is finished, feel free to charge it with the same intention. Something like protection would be a good intention for this Sigil of Michael.

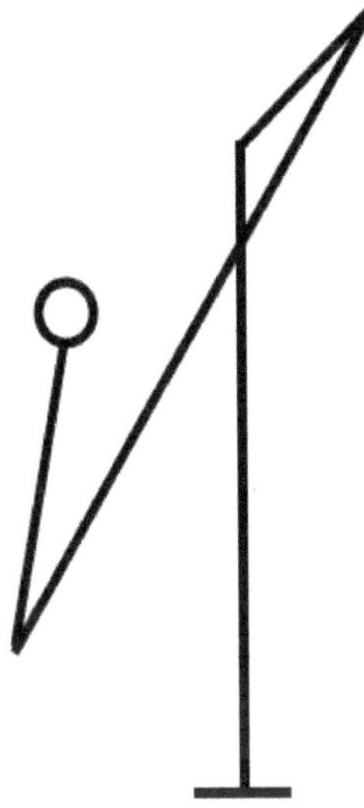

Figure 11.

Now you may have also seen sigils with seemingly cryptic text surrounding them. This is a totally optional step, but it is a fundamental practice that helps you imbue further energy into the Sigil. You essentially draw a ring, or rings, around the Sigil. Within the space between write a word, phrase, or sentences (anything you'd like really). As you write it be sure you continue to focus energy for your intention just as you did when creating the Sigil itself. This is where the extra boost of energy is coming from. You can elect to write this in any language you'd like. Many simply use English, but it is also possible to use any number of ancient languages, or even create your own cipher using

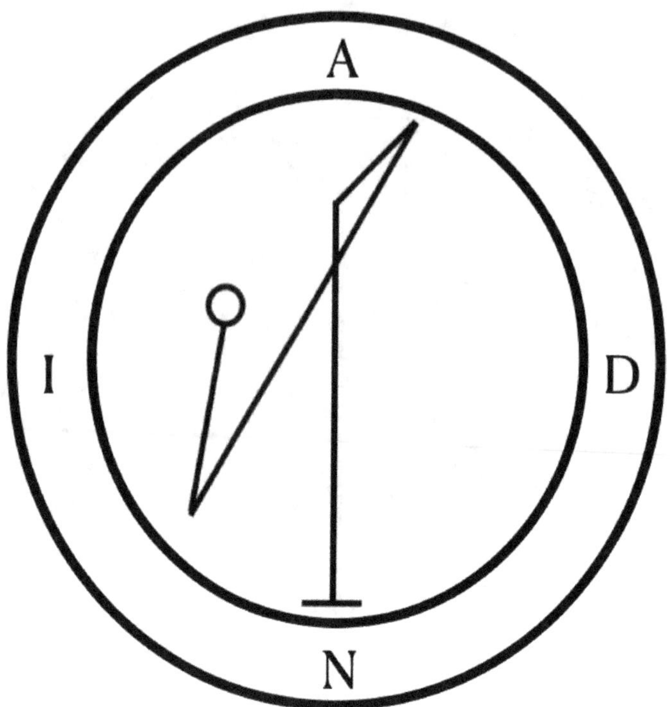

Figure 12.

imagery that is effective for you. Included are two completed examples using English, and the Theban Alphabet. Theban is a substitution cipher for the English Alphabet. Each letter of the alphabet corresponds to a special symbol in Theban. The creation of the Theban Alphabet is still slightly in question with the first formal publication we know of being around 1518 in the "*Polygraphia*". (11)

What we do know however is that the alphabet served as a simple, but effective, method for keeping prying eyes from reading a given work. While the substitution cipher is easily decoded by anyone with the alphabetical key, it does stand to prevent a random passerby from simply reading your work (assuming they don't have the cipher memorized). As such, practitioners of Witchcraft and other practices of magick took to Theban to use as an alphabet for transcribing various things for their traditions.

It is totally optional to make use of Theban, some would rather use their native tongue, or even other ancient languages. What is nice about Theban is that it is akin to hiding in plain sight. It is just obscure enough that other practitioners of magick should be able to figure out what you've written, while everyone else just thinks it looks like scraggly symbols. This makes sharing work and focusing intentions a little more siloed, albeit this is just one application and it is not necessarily of any astute importance to do things this way.

In the previous sample Sigil, the letters *"ADNI"* are written in an even placement around the Sigil in the outer circle. Vowels other than that starting "A" and ending "I" are removed from the word *"Adonai"* for conciseness, placement, and general representation of the original Hebrew transliterated to English. Adonai is for the name of God that you may have noticed when charging the pentagram for Michael during the LBRP and LIRP. You could also write out Michael's name here, but in practice there are different correspondences and complexities regarding Archangels. There are distinct angel's that share the same names even, but have specific governances that are very different. In fact you may intend to utilize the Archangel Michael that corresponds with the element of fire like we are here, rather than the Michael that shares the same name but is the Archangel of Hod on the Tree of Life. The book I've referenced quite a few times called *"Angels and Archangels"* by Damien Echols is an excellent resource to learn more about all the angels and correspondences. It is not the most in depth resource, and isn't intended to be, so further study is recommended. However, it is a powerful resource for anyone jumping into Ceremonial Magick with a focus on working with angels, and I could not recommend it more.

Other works such as *"The 72 Angels of Magick: Instant Access to the Angels of Power (The Gallery of Magick)"* by Damon Brand or *"Book of the Hidden Name - Magick of the Shem HaMephorash Angels"* by Maximus Tyrannus Avery can be used for deeper study. Going back to original Golden Dawn works and seeing how they lay out correspondences is also beneficial. A very useful Tarot deck that was created in recent years also serves as an amazing resource for angel correspondences. It is known as *"Angel Tarot"* by Travis McHenry.

Because of this complexity with various angel names overlapping, and even some correspondences being shared, it is wise to make distinctions for yourself between one Sigil or another. Two Sigils representing Michael may look the same, but if you want to use the symbolism for two distinct purposes, using other correspondences like the name of God, or the element, or even your intent can help differentiate them to your subconscious. In this case *ADNI* corresponds to Michael the archangel of the element of fire. As such it can be used to charge this Sigil further with the proper intent.

In the following sample Sigil the Theban alphabet is used to achieve the same goal, but spells out *"ADNI"* in Theban rather than English. Both are the same, but feel free to make use of any that serve your intended purpose. These can also double as fantastic art pieces, and gifts to loved ones that are accepting of the energy you are placing into these items.

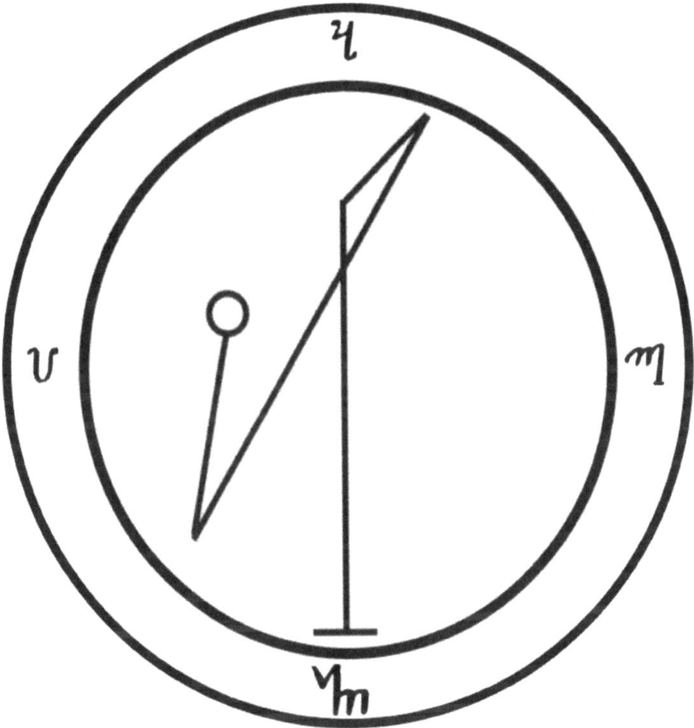

Figure 13.

Rose Cross Sigil Creator (English)

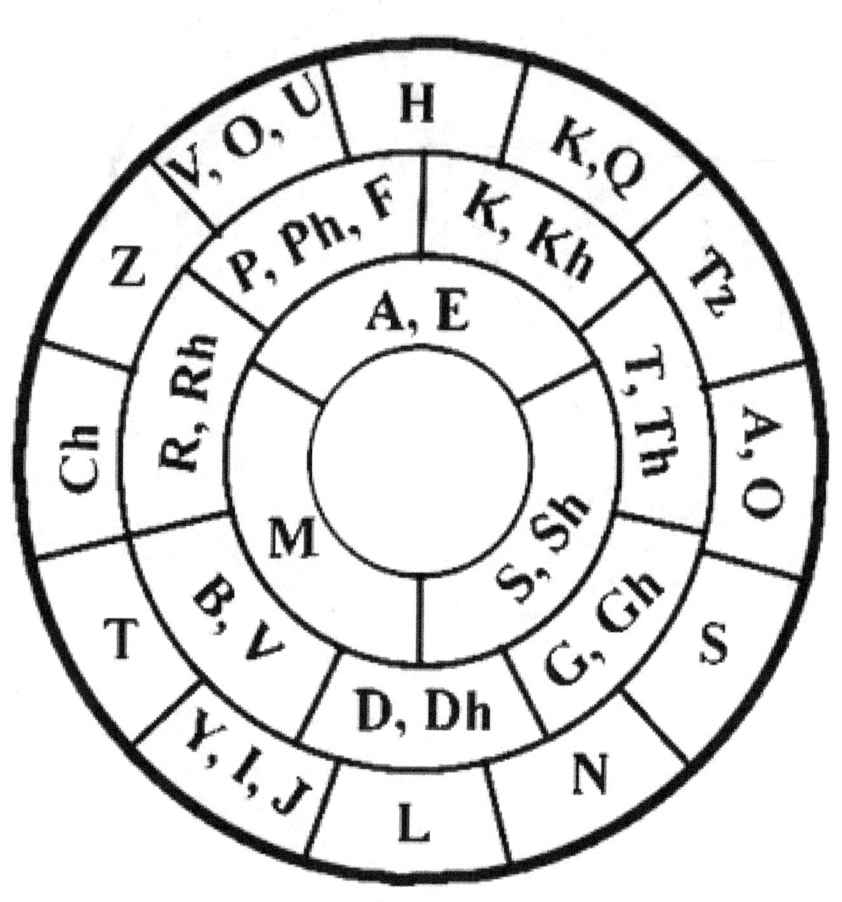

Figure 14.

Rose Cross Sigil Creator (Hebrew)

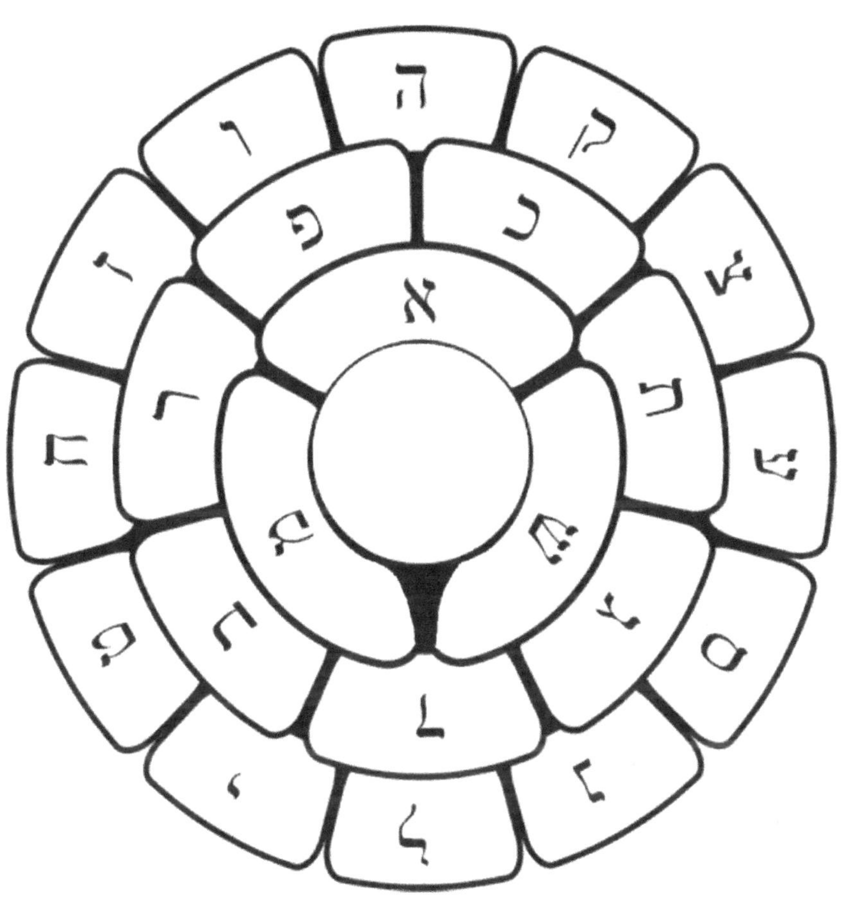

Figure 15.

Crafting Sigils does not require any fancy tooling. That said, some tools that could be beneficial in the practice are as follows:

1. Card Stock - Used to support the weaker paper Sigil for longevity.

2. Linen Paper - Higher quality paper with better structural support.

3. Scissors - For cutting, a straight edge razor could be useful as well for finer cuts.

4. Glue - to glue the linen paper to the card stock.

5. Pigma Micron Pens - Very precise pens that come in a variety of colors which are useful for color correspondence matching.

6. Tracing Paper - To trace sigils over using the provided templates.

7. Circle Templates - Useful templates to assist in drawing more accurate circles. Good for if you wish to draw an outer ring.

Some of those items are a bit on the expensive side, and those without the financial means may not be able to make use of them. This is why it's important to emphasize that this can be done with anything from a pencil and normal paper, to a stick with some sand. Don't get hung up on the physical materials. Focus on the energy and intent you are directing, that is the only thing that really matters. You can have a powerful symbol drawn terribly wrong, but as long as your energy and intention was right, it will still yield some result that you manifested.

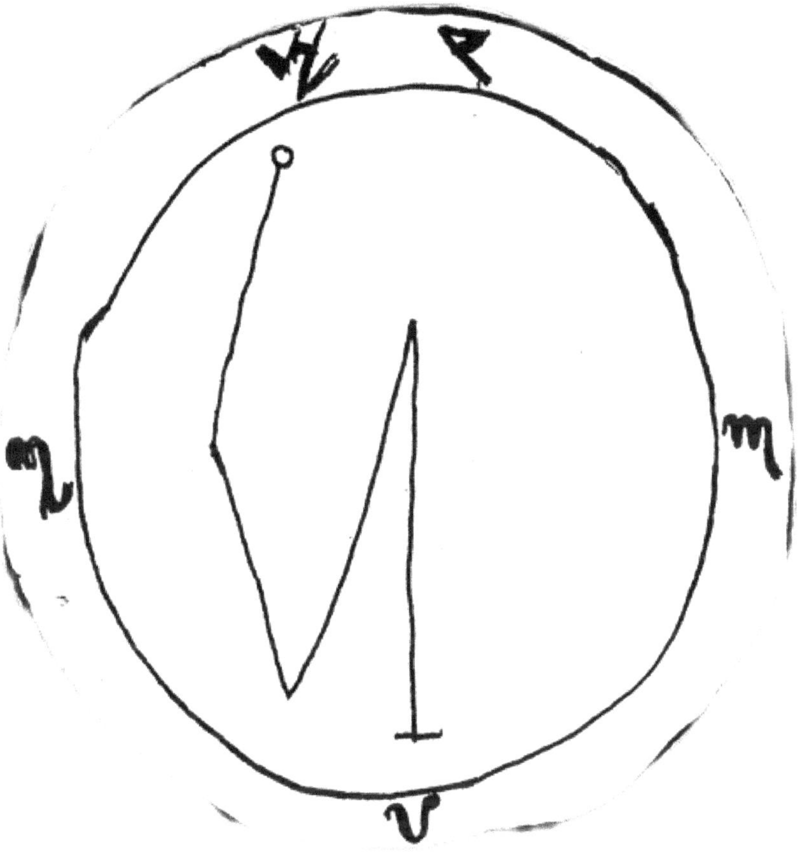

Sigil of Uriel - Handmade and surrounded by the name "Uriel" in Theban

Chapter 14: The Path Forward

At this point you are fully equipped with a strong foundation of fundamentals to use in beginning your own practice. Know that each thing you have done has a breadth and depth of its own. You can quite literally explore each individual practice from every chapter to an infinite degree. Use these practices to explore your true will and identify your path. While not required by any means, the broader you expand your practice into new topics, the more growth you will experience. The majority of growth often comes from obtaining new knowledge and experiencing new things. At some point, as practices become more complex, you might stop learning and simply be doing the work. This is good, there's no reason to stop just because things stop feeling profound, but it is also good in those moments to return to your fundamentals. Good fundamentals teach us not only how, but why we do things the way we do.

In this chapter new, more advanced, practices will be introduced. Everything from rituals, alchemy, divination work, and even guidance on how to expand your practice from here. The ultimate goal of this work is to introduce very complex metaphysical topics in a way that covers the vastness of everything you may want to learn about, or didn't even know you wanted to learn about. While the fundamentals are admittedly lengthy, and require much work and dedication to master, they are not the whole picture. They do define the the foundation of the whole picture, which is why condensing them and encouraging exploration for further learning is so important.

Getting a taste for what you should explore next will hopefully assist you on your personal path. It can be frustrating to finish something and not know where to go next. Let the conclusion of this text be just the mere beginnings of your journey. As above, so below. As within, so without.

Lesser Banishing Ritual of the Hexagram

The next building block of the LBRP is the Lesser Banishing Ritual of the Hexagram (LBRH). There are in fact increasingly more complex rituals that include the "Greater Banishing" or "Greater Invoking" variants of these building blocks. That is something to be aware of, but the LBRH is the immediate next step to begin working through. The LBRH serves the same purpose as the LBRP in terms of preparing a ritual space, but invokes different entities for different purposes in terms of TGW from a broader scale. Specifically you will be working with elemental energies still, but the directionality will be based on planetary correspondence.

1.   Start by performing the full LBRP, but once you return to the center do not conclude the ritual.

2.   Approach the *Eastern* wall again. Visualize the pentagram that is still in that space. Draw a hexagram golden flame using the sword mudra as shown below. They are two overlapping triangles pointing upward. This is the banishing hexagram that corresponds with fire. Note that the numbering on this indicates what side to start for both triangles. You will start at the top one, and immediately to the first step of the second. This will be the same for all hexagrams going forward.

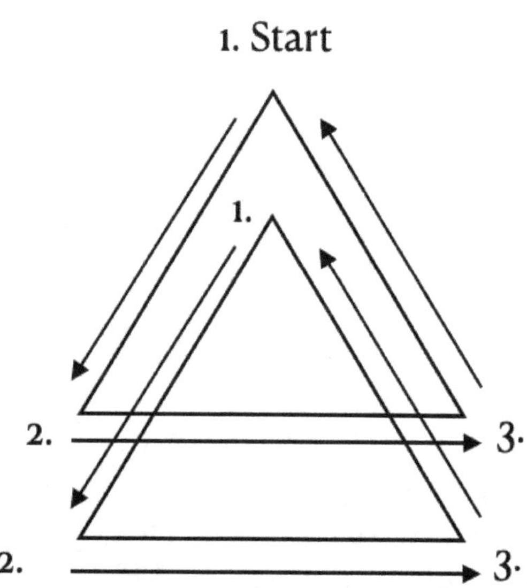

Figure 16.

3. Inhale and place your extended fingers through the center of the hexagram and see it burn brighter just as you did with the LBRP.

4. Now vibrate the mantra *Ararita* (ar-uh-ree-tah). This is an acronym for *"Achad Rosh Achdotho Rosh Ichudo Temurator Achad"*. This is Hebrew for *"One is his beginning, one is his individuality, his permutation is one"*. *Ararita* is used as the mantra to express the meaning of this phrase which is that there is only one source from which all things originate, and everything is that source. Exactly like how "the source" we've defined thus far is just experiencing the universe through us.

5. Inhale again and draw a white line from the East to the Southern wall in your space.

6. Inhale again and draw the next hexagram in golden flame same as before. This hexagram is a normal hexagram and represents earth.

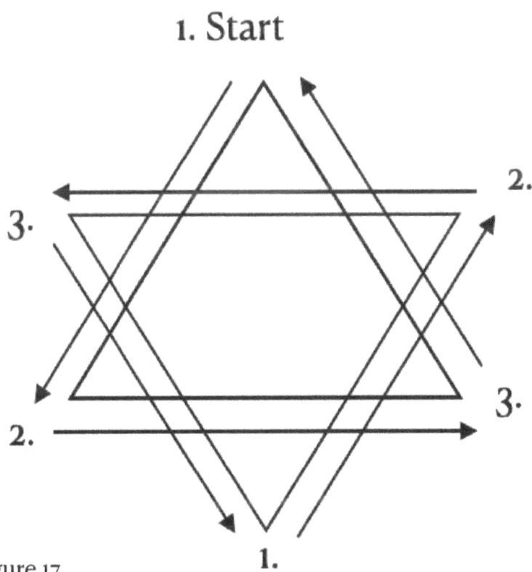

Figure 17.

7.   Charge this hexagram the same way as before.

8.   Inhale and vibrate the mantra *Ararita* once again.

9.   Inhale and draw a white line from the *South* to the *Western* wall.

10. Inhale again and draw the next hexagram in gold flame. This is the hexagram of air. This one is drawn in a diamond shape.

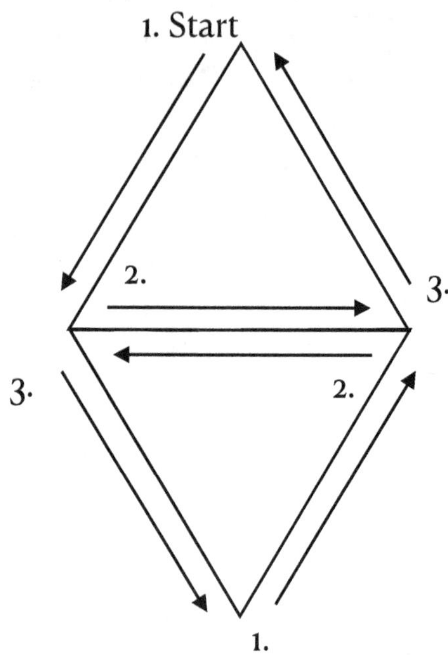

Figure 18.

11. Charge this hexagram just as before.

12. Inhale and vibrate the mantra *Ararita* again. As you may have noticed, this is the primary mantra for this ritual.

13. Draw a white line from the *West* to the *Northern* wall.

14. Inhale and begin to draw the final hexagram in gold flame. This hexagram represents water and is shaped similar to an hourglass with triangles.

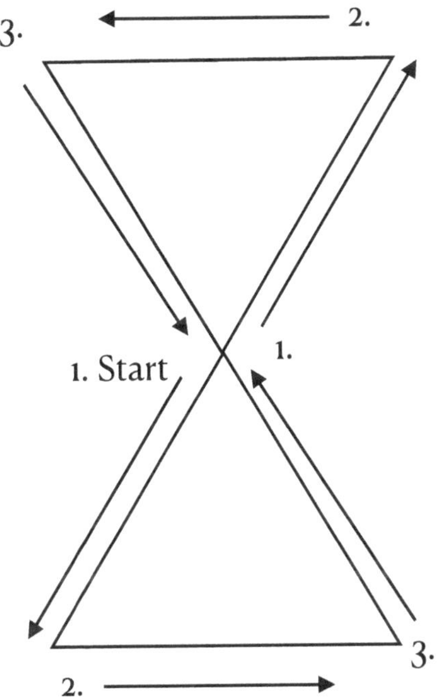

Figure 19.

15. Charge the hexagram as you have been.

16. One last time, vibrate the mantra *Ararita*.

17. Draw a white line back to the Eastern wall to complete the circle.

18. Stand in the middle of your space and close yourself in a sphere of white light just as you did in the LBRP, but there is no need to say any special words. Just envelope yourself in a sphere of white light in the center of your space.

19. Perform The Analysis of the Keyword ritual (LVX).

20. Conclude with the Qabalistic Cross.

Lesser Invoking Ritual of the Hexagram

The Lesser Invoking Ritual of the Hexagram (LIRH) will hopefully come naturally to you. Simply perform the exact same steps as you did in the LBRH, but reverse the direction of drawing in your hexagrams.

1. Start by performing the full LIRP with two caveats. The first being, do not issue instructions to the angels yet, and once you return to the center, do not conclude the ritual.

2. Approach the *Eastern* wall again. Visualize the pentagram that is still in that space. Draw a hexagram golden flame using the sword mudra as shown below. They are two overlapping triangles pointing upward.

This is the invoking hexagram that corresponds with fire. Note that the numbering on this indicates what side to start for both triangles. You will start at the top one, and immediately to the first step of the second. This will be the same for all hexagrams going forward.

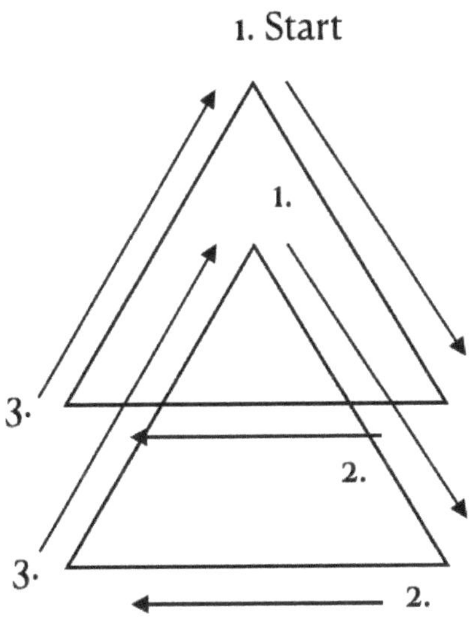

Figure 20.

3. Inhale and place your extended fingers through the center of the hexagram and see it burn brighter just as you did with the LIRP.
4. Now vibrate the mantra *Ararita*.
5. Inhale again and draw a white line from the East to the Southern wall in your space.

6. Inhale again and draw the next hexagram in golden flame like before. This hexagram is a normal hexagram and represents earth.

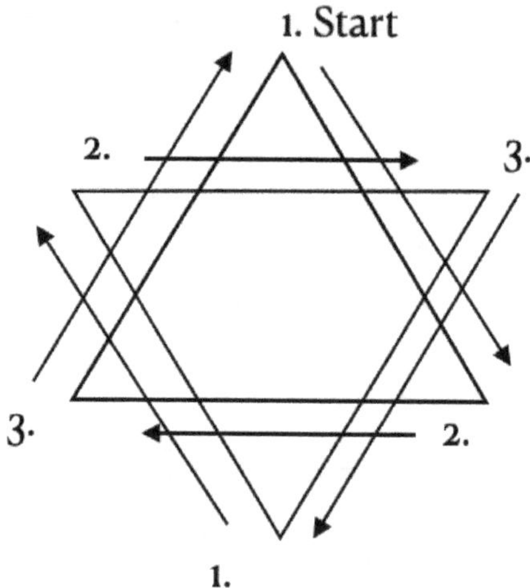

Figure 21.

7. Charge this hexagram the same way as before.
8. Inhale and vibrate the mantra *Ararita* once again.
9. Inhale and draw a white line from the *South* to the *Western* wall.
10. Inhale again and draw the next hexagram in gold flame. This is the hexagram of air. This one is drawn in a diamond shape.

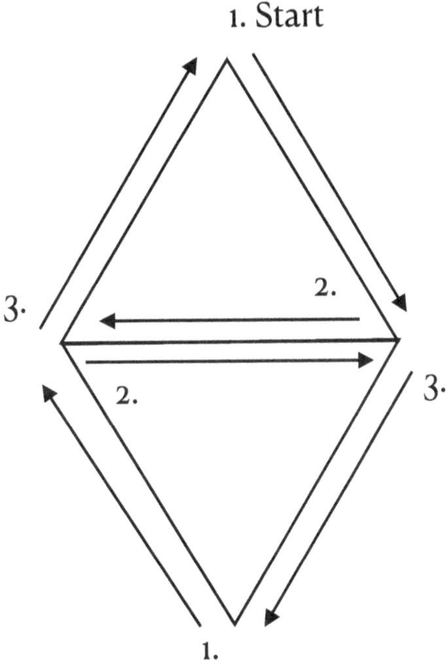

Figure 22.

11. Charge this hexagram just as before.
12. Inhale and vibrate the mantra *Ararita* again. This is the primary mantra for this ritual.
13. Draw a white line from the *West* to the *Northern* wall.
14. Inhale and begin to draw the final hexagram in gold flame. This hexagram represents water and is shaped similar to an hourglass with triangles.

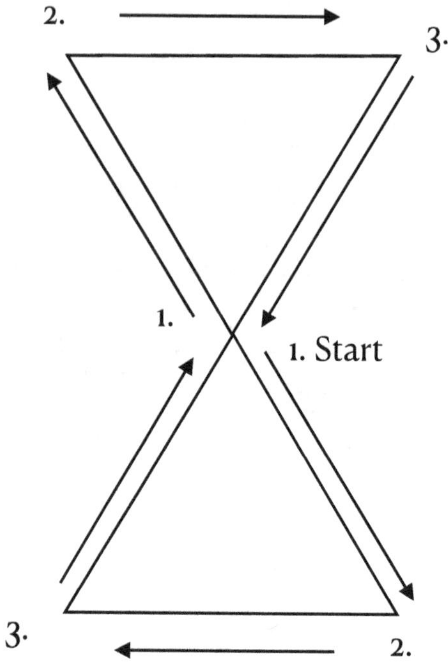

Figure 23.

15. Charge the hexagram as you have been.
16. One last time, vibrate the mantra *Ararita*.
17. Draw a white line back to the Eastern wall to complete the circle.
18. Stand in the middle of your space and close yourself in a sphere of white light just as you did in the LBRP, but there is no need to say any special words. Just envelope yourself in a sphere of white light in the center of your space.
19. Perform The Analysis of the Keyword ritual (LVX).

20. Issue your prayer, instructions, or manifestations like your would for the LIRP to each angel.

21. Conclude with the Qabalistic Cross.

Divination

Divination is commonly seen as a way to see into the future, usually through some sort of spiritual or otherwise supernatural means. In Ceremonial Magick this is still sort of true, but it is a bit more nuanced than that. Divination can help you gain an idea of what is coming next, but remember, as a Ceremonial Magickian, you control your will. This means the only "future" divination can predict is the one you are crafting. In this way divination is more of a reflection of the path you are already on. It is a way to read into things that have happened, things that are happening, and things that will happen. The only way to understand the results of a divination exercise is to understand yourself and connect what is being reflected to your own experience.

There are many divination tools from the Tarot, Scrying, Bibliomancy, reading palms, and even tea leaves. In Ceremonial Magick you are free to apply any of these techniques, as with anything else. While you will commonly see heavy practice of these techniques in realms of Natural Magick, many of them are founded in Ceremonial Magick, and have been refined over the years. Regardless of their origin and place in magick, divination can be a powerful tool to assist in self reflection and carving your path.

Tarot

The Tarot is a set of cards that is used heavily in divination across all practices. There are many decks with many purposes, but it all actually started as a card game in 15th century Italy. The game was later adapted around the 18th century to be used in the practice of cartomancy. There are many tools and practices for cartomancy, you can even use a plain deck of playing cards, and map correspondences. Tarot simply became one of the most widely known and popular. While Tarot was not initially started as a divination tool, it has been heavily refined, with various correspondences mapped over the years. This has proved extremely useful in practice by many divination practitioners.

There are many decks for the Tarot, but as a beginner, using the Rider-Waite deck is a good place to start. Usually when you purchase a Tarot deck like the Rider-Waite it will actually come with a little instruction booklet on various ways to conduct Tarot readings. Some traditions say you must be gifted your first Tarot deck before purchasing or creating others, or else it won't work, or worse be cursed. This isn't based in any fact, however it is a fun tradition to gift a Tarot deck if you have any loved ones that are interested.

Below three basic methods for reading the Tarot for divination purposes are provided. These are the most fundamental and basic types of readings, but they are all encompassing for something any starting practitioner of divination might want to peer into about themselves. You can also perform readings for others, but keep in mind, at least in Ceremonial Magick, these readings are a reflection of the individual. You can only really truly predict things they already know about themselves and use the cards to derive the next step they'll likely take on their path. This is powerful for those who are not practicing any sort of focused spiritual path, because they may not reflect on their life very often. Especially not the present, as so many of us are simply not truly present. This forces them to look inward, and through that introspection, understand why the past, present, and future are laid out the way they are. This is true of your own readings as well. A Tarot reading's outcomes are never permanent, especially for a Ceremonial Magickian. This is because if we see a future we don't like, and it's not aligning with our will, we can use our reflection of the present to change the future outcome that is expected. Sound familiar?

Hopefully it does. This is exactly what was introduced at the very start of this text when describing what it means to be in control of your reality, and responses to the world around you. Remember, the future is simply the present you haven't experienced yet, and the past was the present you experienced at one point. All there ever truly will be is the present moment, and even if you're in the midst of it, you can always choose the way you respond.

Before you begin each of these be sure to thoroughly shuffle and cut the deck of cards. Once you have done so perform the following steps:

1. Hold your hand over the top of the deck of cards and close your eyes.

2. Inhale and see white light come down from above. Direct this light to saturate the deck of cards.

3. Inhale again and vibrate the mantra *HRU* (hee-rooh). These letters are all that's left of the archangel's name that resides over the Tarot. The rest has currently been lost to time, but fortunately this is more than enough to call upon this entity for a blessing over our deck.

4. As you vibrate the mantra see the deck glow brighter and brighter.

5. Now say the following prayer, feel free to adapt it if need be, this is simply a good starter prayer: *"HRU bless this deck. Give me the ability to understand that which I do not know, and derive meaning from what I observe. Let this be for my (or other person's Name) benefit. Amen."*

6. Now open your eyes and begin to perform one of the card drawing techniques.

Single Card Draw:

1. Draw a single card from the top of the deck. Reflect on what it means. Use the correspondence that came with your book if you wish. Another great reference book for mapping angels and correspondences to the Tarot is once again, Angels and Archangels, by Damien Echols. It contains a list of all the cards, the angel correspondences, and what they mean in a concise format.

2. Once you have researched and reflected on what it means, internalize the meaning. This single card draw is reflecting your current state in the present moment and is telling you where you are. More precisely it is addressing something you may or may not be aware of about the current state in your life. By reflecting on this,

the end result would be to make you aware and understanding of this situation. This provides clarity so you may move forward with focused knowledge on something you may not have otherwise been privy to.

Two Card Draw:

1. This card draw is a little different. Feel free to draw two cards directly from the top of the deck, or spread them out in front of you and pick two at random. This is where intuition comes in a little. If you choose to spread them out then stick with whatever you naturally touch first, don't second guess, just go with whatever you naturally are drawn to first try.

2. Place the first card you picked face up before you on your left, and the second face up on your right.

3. Now just like before, reflect and research the correspondence of each card. In time you'll begin to memorize the different meanings, but there are 72 cards and a myriad of different decks. Don't expect yourself to be able to do this work without a reference any time soon, that is totally normal!

4. This time the card on your left represents something you are doing that you need to let go of and move on from. The card on your right represents something you need to begin moving towards as you move away from the other circumstance.

Three Card Draw:

1. Similar to the two card draw you can either draw the top three cards, or spread them out and pick at random.

2. Place the first card on your left, the second in the center, and the third to your right, all face up.

3. In this drawing the card to your left is a reflection of your past. This card will tell you what you used to do in a particular context based on the card's correspondence. The middle card will reflect your current state in the present moment. The card to your right reflects the current state of the future path you are headed towards. This is a basic prediction, but it lays out your full timeline to give you context regarding where you've been, where you are, and where you are headed based on where you are.

Tarot can be both a fun and insightful medium for divination. As you become more familiar and comfortable with it try adding different drawing techniques and experimenting with different decks.

Bibliomancy

Bibliomancy is a more straightforward, yet arguably more complex form of divination. Bibliomancy is used purely for reflection of your current state, for gaining insight into the present moment. In a way this too can be used to read the future, but really that's only true on a case by case basis depending on what you see reflected, and your interpretation of that. This can't really be used to work with others, but you may try if you can sort out how to direct the intention of energy on behalf of someone else. At that point I'd simply use the Tarot, but if you find it to be valuable to observe Bibliomancy instead go for it!

In either case Bibliomancy is essentially the process of randomly opening a book to a page, blindly placing your finger down, and reading one or two sentences based on wherever it lands. Using this sentence you'll apply the meaning to yourself and use your intuition, and psychic perception, to understand what insight you are gaining. Commonly people use The Bible for Bibliomancy, hence the name, but you can use any book you'd like. Some people say the book must naturally fall open, whether it falls from a shelf, or you drop it purposefully. Unfortunately, unless you're using a very old book, or don't care about damaging a book, this doesn't work super well all the time. Simply opening a book at random is just as effective in practice. A quick step by step of how to perform this technique is as follows:

1. Select a book to use. Using The Bible to start with is wise, but not required by any means. Place the book in front of you.

2. Close your eyes and open the book. You can choose to drop it and let it fall open, or simply open it randomly with your eyes closed.

3. Keeping your eyes closed, place your finger down randomly on a page that is opened.

4. Open your eyes and begin reading where your finger was placed. If you started at the beginning of a sentence then start there, if you started in the middle and it's not quite clear, try starting from the beginning of that sentence. Starting at the end of a sentence would follow the same principle of reverting back to the beginning, but if you'd like, regardless of placement, feel free to incorporate the line before or after (or both). Try not to over do it though. If it's not making sense to you initially, adding context won't help, because at that point you would just be reading the text, and not applying it to

yourself. For this reason, single sentence reading is the most straightforward, but it doesn't hurt to read on a little more. The important thing is to focus your intention on self reflection, and attempt to understand what the words before you mean to *you*.

Bibliomancy, while clearly simple to do in practice, takes a lot of intuition and self reflection. It is simple and easy on the surface, but the actual divination portion can be incredibly difficult to understand sometimes. If you find yourself not deriving much, just keep practicing. Even try different books, and change your focus. Without this, it's no more than reading a random sentence from a random book.

Divination as a whole is not something everyone is particularly gifted in. That said, it is absolutely something anyone can do. It just means as a practice that it is a little more difficult to tap into intuition for some, where it is natural for others. I find the Tarot to be beneficial for those with less draw to divination as a practice, since you can incorporate the archangel of the Tarot to assist you. This helps get into the right headspace for such practices.

Alchemy

Alchemy is a strange concept, and when you see that word you may begin to picture images of large glass vials, and strange heating contraptions. These are actually still valid tools in the alchemical process to this day, but alchemy isn't what you might think it is in the context of Ceremonial Magick. Traditionally, alchemy is a process used to figure out different formulas for purifying various materials. The goal of this purification process was to change the chemical structure of a given material so that it becomes pure gold.

As a result of this more chemistry focused approach, many who practiced alchemy later transitioned to the field of chemistry, and since then the practice has mostly died outside of esotericism and historical research. In Ceremonial Magick however, the practice continues. This is because while physical in nature, alchemist of the past were aiming to not only achieve a goal of turning various things to gold, but also a way to purify oneself. In other terms, alchemy was equally spiritually motivated as it was scientifically. The symbol of an alchemist is one you may have heard of, the philosopher's stone. This was a theoretical object that if created, or identified via other means, was meant to help one achieve enlightenment.

You may have understood this object at some point as a stone that helped one to achieve immortality. This is equally as true. The key piece of knowledge taught by Ceremonial Magick is, that goal wasn't simply to become immortal for the sake of never dying. Rather, becoming immortal was a tool to help one live indefinitely, so they might almost guarantee the completion of TGW in this lifetime. Essentially the fear of death halting one's progress to achieving TGW drove some alchemist magickians to seek this object.

Ceremonial Magick emphasizes the metaphorical process that alchemy represents. Rather than pining over the philosopher's stone, Ceremonial Magick focuses inward on TGW, and uses the practical aspects only if one desires. Essentially the entire process you are going through as you practice Ceremonial Magick is one that can be described as alchemical. We are purifying our spirit over and over and over again until we eventually achieve our true will. As alluded to, this metaphorical approach does not come without some interesting avenues for practical application. Those Ceremonial Magickians that choose to practice alchemy do so by implementing some of the practical concepts into their spiritual work.

For example, one may purify some sort of extract from rose petals using alcohol. The idea here would be to take the energy and correspondence represented by the rose petals, then use the physical alchemical process to create a tincture that is the pure essence of those correspondences. This is because after the alcohol purifies the materials, what remains is a tincture containing the essence and intention of what you created. These tinctures can be crafted in a way that is purely representational, but also something like blue lotus could be used to produce a reactionary effect of calmness and focus. Tinctures are just one way to observe the alchemical process. We'll expound more on tinctures in the next section, but you can also perform simple alchemy by making teas, making spell jars, and even cooking!

When it comes to the fundamentals of what alchemy is and isn't in Ceremonial Magick, it is actually quite straightforward. If you are purifying something for a specific intention, it is likely alchemy, even if it's just spiritual alchemy. In this way all Ceremonial Magickians are at least spiritual alchemist. Much like divination, and some of the other practices in this section, alchemy is not a requirement for any practitioner. However, as a means to introduce as many fundamentals as possible in this text, it could be of great benefit for those who wish to incorporate this practice into their work.

Tinctures

Tinctures are a simple and effective way to begin doing alchemy in your practice. A tincture is created by mixing alcohol or vinegar with a given herb or other digestible material. Keep in mind, you don't necessarily fully drink tinctures. Most people place a drop on or under their tongue when using them. That said, it is going into your body even at a small amount, so keep that in mind when selecting your ingredients. For alcohol, using off the shelf spirits is actually something that is not only possible, but recommended. It is advised to use a more neutral spirit like vodka, but generally speaking anything that is 20% ABV (40 proof) will work. Food grade ethyl alcohol is also a standard to make use of, just make sure it meets the same proof criteria.

If you are averse to alcohol for any reason, vinegar will also be a valid option. The ratios are a little different depending on whether you use dried or fresh herbs. The ratios for each will be provided below. Be sure to experiment and try different ratios and herbs to see what works for you!

1. Gather your materials and get yourself organized. You will need your herbs or material of choice, your

alcohol or vinegar, and an airtight container to keep the tincture in.

2. Wash and coarsely chop the herbs.

3. Place the herbs into your container.

4. Pour your alcohol or vinegar into the container. For fresh herbs pour 1:1 alcohol or vinegar. For example if you have 1 ounce of herbs, use 1 ounce of alcohol or vinegar. With dry herbs use a 1:4 ratio, so for every 1 ounce of herbs, pour 4 ounces of alcohol or vinegar.

5. Seal the airtight container. Optionally, bless it with the intention that your material represents to give it more energy.

6. Let the mixture sit for 6 weeks, shake it occasionally every day or two. It may take a little more or less time. You'll know it's likely done if the material you are purifying is washed out in color, and the liquid within has been infused with that color from the material.

7. Once it is ready, open the jar and strain the liquid into a new container so the solid materials are removed from the mixture. You may do whatever you'd like with the left over material waste. Some common things might be to burn them ceremonially, add them to a compost, or even use them to create other things. You could use them in food, or even making topical ointments. This depends on what herbs you used, but researching similar ideas can help you determine what to do with the waste.

Now that you have your tincture, simply drop 1-3 drops on or underneath your tongue and let it set. Observe how it makes you feel. If you made a tincture for a specific intention, say for happiness, you can place that under your tongue before performing the LIRP, and focus your LIRP on that intention of happiness as well. In this way the tincture is adding more energy to your ritual work and helping you focus and feel that intention through its physical properties, as well as its energetic correspondences.

Natural Magick

Not all Natural Magick is alchemy, but what will be suggested below are practices that are, or at least could be considered, alchemical in nature. As a quick recap, Natural Magick is simply magick that deals with physical aspects of reality more so than working with spirits and deities. Practitioners of Natural Magick may work with various spiritual entities, and even worship deities, but the mechanisms by which they do so are often via physical mediums. For example, alchemy. Here are some Natural Magick tools, and some fundamental examples you can try that make use of those tools.

1. Crystals - Crystals are a vast topic in and of themselves, so much so that they have bled into popular culture. Just like everything in the observable universe, crystals can have correspondences and energetic associations that can be made use of in magickal practices. Some common crystals you may want to work with starting out are as follows:
    + Amethyst: Calming and Tranquility
    + Citrine: Restoration and Cleansing
    + Jade: Balance, Luck, and Prosperity
    + Rose Quartz: Love and Peace
    + Lapis Lazuli: Clarity, Truth, and Communication

2. Herbalism - In modernity herbalist are often focused on creating medicines from various plants. This is applicable in Natural Magick as well, but it's not just about medicine in the sense of how we might interpret it at the time of this text. Instead, working with herbs also has many other benefits, just like with crystals. Various plants have different correspondences of course, with a very large variety, but here are a few examples to get started with:

+ Blue Lotus (Herbal Smoking or in a Tea): For wisdom, intelligence, and spiritual focus.
+ Mint (Chewed or in a Tea): For healing, luck, and protection.
+ Lavender (Herbal Smoking or in a Tea): For protection, purification, and tranquility.

3. Spell Jars - Spell jars come in all shapes and sizes, but their purpose is the same regardless of construction. A spell jar is a physical representation of an intention you wish to manifest. Within a spell jar you can place various herbs, crystals, and any other materials you wish. Essentially you want to mix whatever correspondences you need to achieve your intention. This is done by adding in the materials that map to those correspondences. Some practitioners elect to use a jar and seal it, then leave it in their home somewhere as a meditation focus and reminder. Others may construct a jar that a candle can be burned in so that way the contents inside are slowly burned away, and the energy for your intention is released into the world. There's really no wrong way to make a spell jar. These work a lot like tinctures in terms of construction, but with even less requirements and rules. You can mix

everything from sand, salt, rose petals, mint, wood, steel, and even tincture essence if you so choose. Some common spell jars and their ingredients are as follows:

✦ Love: Honey, Alcohol, Rose Petals, Patchouli, Rose Quartz, Himalayan Salt.

✦ Focus or Intelligence: Blue Lotus, Lapis Lazuli, Frankincense, Mint, Sea Salt.

✦ Wealth: Jade, Ginger, Thyme, Celtic Sea Salt.

These Natural Magick practices are just the tip of the iceberg. What is fortunate about Natural Magick is that there are a vast number of resources. Thanks to Wicca, and a lot of modern natural healing movements, we now have hundreds of books, articles, and even online stores that exist. These mediums carry information and products on everything from tinctures, to crystals, and even spell jars. The beauty of Natural Magick is in all of the options and paths you can take to achieve the same goal in a single practice. This gives you even more room to create tools in your practice that are unique to you, while maintaining an accurate correspondence to what we currently understand about the world. Incorporating these practices into Ceremonial Magick can help provide an extra physical experience to enhance a given practice. None if it is necessary, but it is beneficial, and can even be quite fun. Magick always has some fun underneath, as it should. While there is a lot of hard work involved, ultimately it is to your benefit to achieve your will. If you have fun along the way, it is because that is what you put into the universe, and it is simply reflecting that back to you.

Astrology

Astrology has a strong place in Ceremonial Magick. Like many of the practices that have been uncovered and adapted into the work of Ceremonial Magick, astrology is an ancient study that we can find across many cultures throughout the world's history. Modern astrology teaches many concepts that still resonate with Ceremonial Magick, however, it simply does not go deep enough. Modern astrology takes liberties that are not applicable to Ceremonial Magick. Many modern readings and divination practices, like horoscopes, are very generic and surface level. That doesn't make them useless or untrue, but they are simply not what Ceremonial Magick uses astrology for.

To provide further context, analyzing one's birth chart to figure out their various zodiacal associations in life is a valuable practice both in Ceremonial Magick, and in modern astrological divination. That said, often modern astrology takes these correspondences at face value to determine a conclusion. Thanks to the generic nature of the modern practice, this may yield mixed results with individuals who carve their paths differently in life. For example, someone born under the astrological sign Leo may in fact display traits of a Leo by modern standards. This individual could be confident, intelligent, and driven. However, in this same context, Leo's are often associated with being extroverted, the center of attention, and even prideful. In this example, that same person could exhibit the traits of confidence, but be introverted. They could be confident, but very humble. Most modern astrology just leaves a lot of room for interpretation, which often means it is very accurate, but with the caveat that one must pick and choose what applies to them, or simply accept it as a whole sale truth. The only problem with the latter part of this analysis is that accepting something that tells you who you are, rather than defining who you are on your own, is in direct conflict with one's true will.

It is up to you to decide who you are, and how you wish to respond to the world. No birth chart or planetary correspondence can define that if you are a Ceremonial Magickian. Keep in mind, this isn't a derogatory stance against modern astrology. Modern astrology affords many benefits, and is almost necessary in some ways to keep astrology as a practice alive. It is simply that Ceremonial Magick defines and views astrology in a different lens that isn't quite fully compatible with what one might see in a pop culture article on it in the era this text was written in.

Ceremonial Magick uses astrology in a majorly important way that can help you determine not only how you came into this world, but also the path you are taking out of it. Using the Leo example again, but in the context of Ceremonial Magick. One who is born in correspondence with the constellation of Leo, came into this world through that constellation. Not necessarily literally, but in terms of how the universe was aligned astrologically, their birth corresponds to this pathway. This is beneficial to understand, because when you achieve TGW, you are reversing this process to get back to "the source". If you came in through the constellation of Leo, you'll exit through it as well. It is simply the context of which you were born, and astrology is a tool that helps us form a sort of universal map. Using this map we can walk backwards to achieve TGW.

It is important to note that there is nothing special you have to focus on in order to walk back. Practicing Ceremonial Magick, and growing to achieve your true will is going to inevitably guide you where you must go to achieve TGW. You don't have to plan out a specific ritual that has to be conducted around the time of your birth to help you launch yourself into enlightenment. You may want to if you think such a practice would be powerful for your work, but it in no way is relevant outside of your own personal growth and choices. Rather, what understanding this map provides is a deeper understanding of yourself in this current life, based on what correspondences align with your creation.

This is where modern astrology and Ceremonial Magick aim at the same target. Both are simply trying to help us understand ourselves, Ceremonial Magick is looking beyond the surface to apply these concepts, rather than just taking them at face value. As you grow deeper into the various hexagram rituals, you will begin to work with more and more planetary magick. This is the next step, after you have balanced the elements of the Earth. You will then begin to balance the planets, and their alignment with the universe. This includes the stars, various moons, and all of their positions and alignment in the universe. All of these physical things cause a natural and logical energetic reaction in the universe. Even if we don't see a difference in our physical reality, the rotation of a given planet has an energetic impact in general. We know this is true because we know it is exerting some sort of energy to carry out this movement. With Ceremonial Magick we tap into that and are able to expound on it further. This is where all the correspondences come into play.

We know, for example, that Mars is often associated with war, aggression, confidence, and strength. Mars corresponds to Aries and sometimes even Scorpio in a zodiacal context. Using this correspondence, one can utilize the energies of Mars as an Aries or Scorpio to map to their own true will. If you take this understanding of what corresponds to your creation, you can meditate on it and gain a better understanding of how you got here, and for what purpose. Of course balance is necessary to encompass and interact with the entirety of "the source". Without balance we simply focus on ourselves, not the whole of what we are aiming to achieve. As a result, someone who is an Aries shouldn't just focus on working with the energies of Mars, but all planetary energies. Mars would just provide a contextual medium that corresponds with that individual on a somewhat personal level.

To help with identifying the different correspondences, a list of planets and zodiacal references is provided below. Planetary magick outside of the LBRH is a slightly more advanced topic not meant for this text. It is however, your next step, so providing material to get you there is certainly beneficial. Even the LBRH still deals with elemental energies of Earth, but it does so in a way that is more focused on the planetary mediums. Because of this, later hexagram rituals you may learn are heavily reliant on the idea of planetary correspondences with angels. This will begin to launch you into planetary magick in your practice.

Zodiacal Correspondences

1. Aries - Mars
    - ✦ Confidence, aggression, sexuality, and strength.
2. Taurus - Venus
    - ✦ Balance, beauty, affection, and pleasure.
3. Gemini - Mercury
    - ✦ Communication, knowledge, commerce, and exploration.
4. Cancer - Earth's Moon
    - ✦ Divination, dreams, emotions, and self-discovery.
5. Leo - Sun
    - ✦ Prosperity, growth, confidence, and truth.
6. Virgo - Mercury
    - ✦ Communication, knowledge, commerce, and exploration.
7. Libra - Venus
    - ✦ Balance, beauty, affection, and pleasure.
8. Scorpio - Pluto (or Mars)
    - ✦ Renewal, destruction, truth, and discovery.
    - ✦ (Confidence, aggression, sexuality, and strength.)
9. Sagittarius - Jupiter
    - ✦ Growth, prosperity, luck, and justice.
10. Capricorn - Saturn
    - ✦ Immortality, health, law, death, and fate.
11. Aquarius - Uranus (or Saturn)
    - ✦ Intelligence, discovery, individuality, and enlightenment.
    - ✦ (Immortality, health, law, death, and fate.)
12. Pisces - Neptune (or Jupiter)

- ✦ Imagination, creativity, healing, and divination.
- ✦ (Growth, prosperity, luck, and justice.)

You might have noticed that some of the Zodiac is associated, or ruled by, potentially two planets. This is a simple, but important to understand, situation. As the Zodiac was being identified through history, the ancient astrologers were mapping the perceived energetic correspondences to the planets and placement of all things in the observable universe. Over time they mapped these things to this idea of the Zodiac. The keyword in all of that explanation is "observable", because these astrologers didn't have the tools we have today to see as far out as they may have liked. As a result, they used what they could factually observe, and had to make educated assumptions based on this knowledge to tie up loose ends.

This was done to baseline a system of study that became what we call astrology today. Over time we developed technologies that have allowed us to see much deeper into space and the surrounding universe. As a result, we discovered more stars, more planets in our own solar system, more galaxies, and even some best guess calculations for what the odds are of other Earth-like planets to exist within other solar systems.

This has required astrologers to rethink the zodiacal system through time. This change in technology forces astrologers to essentially fully start over their analysis nearly from scratch. If we fail to remove a certain correspondence that we believe in our heart and soul to be true, then we may never see what may have been missed. We simply know more today than we did before, and that will hopefully always be true. Taking a second look when new information is gathered. Being prepared to rethink the existing structure from scratch is not only wise, but necessary. Unfortunately there are different schools of thought when it comes to how to handle the information growth. Some are afraid to change things too much when we have a system that works. Some are afraid we may remake a system that doesn't work to a full potential, because what we know has changed things too much. Some however, are excited for the change, and work really hard to continue to refine astrology. Some unfortunately even in this camp, rush into changes and cause controversial correspondences that lack enough backing to truly make that decision.

No one in either camp is right or wrong, as all acknowledge the fact of change, or at least seem to. If that is true, then it is simply a response to how they wish to acknowledge that change. The fact is the current system seems to work, so not straying from the path before we fully understand the new system is actually smart. The only exception would be if you actually cared to help progress a change to meet further the understanding. Then you take a risk of contribution, because it could take up much of your life to finish that contribution.

In all, the important thing to take away is that what we know now, is all we know. If a Zodiac has two correspondences that are worth noting, it means that as far as we can tell, either correspondence is valid and works for that given idea or intention. All this information is just for some history, and your benefit to make informed decisions on how you wish to use the correspondences. The reality is, when you see them again later on in your practice, you'll be able to easily understand how these ideas fit into Ceremonial Magick. You'll already have a reference for what they are, and what ideas they align with at a zodiacal and planetary level.

Guide Yourself

If you have gotten this far and truly worked through the provided fundamentals then you are ready to take the next step on your path. This step is entirely up to you, you must guide yourself. This is not to say you now have learned all you need to learn, but you have equipped yourself to grow into whatever you choose to learn next. Dive into that next book, dig deeper into divination, energy work, or even sigil work. Whatever you feel is next for you, it is now time to go deeper and evolve your personal practice.

In this section you will be provided with information on how rituals are constructed. Using this information you will be able to begin modifying, adapting, and creating rituals of your own to use in your practice. While you have only started down this path, you are now in a position to truly make it your path. Additionally, what to expect next regarding carrying out your true will is going to be expounded on a bit further to assist you as you progress forward.

Constructing Rituals

Before you can begin constructing rituals, you must understand why a ritual works the way it does. For this example we will break down the LBRP in as detailed terms as possible, hopefully without going unnecessarily deep to give you room to explore further. Using the break down of the LBRP, an example of a custom ritual will be provided that you can use as a reference to begin creating your own based on this formula. Once you fully understand this concept, go and learn more about the other rituals you have conducted and see where you can customize them, or add them to another aspect of your practice.

LBRP Deconstructed

1. Qabalistic Cross:
    1. Purpose - Seals in our aura.
    2. How - Via calling on "the source" and visualizing yourself being enveloped in it. In further context it also connects "the source" to the Earth to synchronize "above" and "below" so you may influence both realms. In this case that influence is to provide protection and seal your aura. This is vocalized by the prayer you vibrate as you conduct the ritual.
2. Facing East:
    1. Purpose - To evoke the element of air associated with the archangel Raphael.
    2. How - The cardinal direction of East is associated with spring and new beginnings. Raphael is also associated with spring, as is the element of air. Knowing these correspondences allow one to combine them in order to begin facing East to evoke Raphael.
3. Evoking Raphael

1. Purpose - To evoke the entity known as the archangel Raphael. The distinct purpose for evoking Raphael is determined by the practitioner, but at a base level you are evoking the elemental associations for each cardinal direction. Raphael is the medium for getting in touch with these energies.
        2. How - By chanting the mantra *YHVH* we evoke a name of God that corresponds to the element of air, and later on, place Raphael to guard that direction when evoked.
4. Facing South:
        1. Purpose - To evoke the element of fire associated with the archangel Michael.
        2. How - The cardinal direction of South is associated with summer and energy of heat. Michael is also associated with summer, as is the element of fire. Knowing these correspondences allow one to combine them in order to begin facing South to evoke Michael.
5. Evoking Michael
        1. Purpose - To evoke the entity known as the archangel Michael. The distinct purpose for evoking Michael is determined by the practitioner, but at a base level you are evoking the elemental associations for each cardinal direction. Michael is the medium for getting in touch with these energies.
        2. How - By chanting the mantra *ADNI* we evoke a name of God that corresponds to the element of fire, and later on, place Michael to guard that direction when evoked.

6. Facing West:
    1. Purpose - To evoke the element of water associated with the archangel Gabriel.
    2. How - The cardinal direction of West is associated with fall and release to make room for new beginnings. Gabriel is also associated with fall, as is the element of water. Knowing these correspondences allow one to combine them in order to begin facing South to evoke Gabriel.
7. Evoking Gabriel
    1. Purpose - To evoke the entity known as the archangel Gabriel. The distinct purpose for evoking Gabriel is determined by the practitioner, but at a base level you are evoking the elemental associations for each cardinal direction. Gabriel is the medium for getting in touch with these energies.
    2. How - By chanting the mantra *AHIH* we evoke a name of God that corresponds to the element of water, and later on, place Gabriel to guard that direction when evoked.
8. Facing North:
    1. Purpose - To evoke the element of earth associated with the archangel Uriel.
    2. How - The cardinal direction of North is associated with fall and introspection and resourcefulness. Uriel is also associated with winter, as is the element of earth. Knowing these correspondences allow one to combine them in order to begin facing South to evoke Uriel.
9. Evoking Uriel

1.   Purpose - To evoke the entity known as the archangel Uriel. The distinct purpose for evoking Uriel is determined by the practitioner, but at a base level you are evoking the elemental associations for each cardinal direction. Gabriel is the medium for getting in touch with these energies.

2.   How - By chanting the mantra *AGLA* we evoke a name of God that corresponds to the element of earth, and later on, place Uriel to guard that direction when evoked.

10. Drawing the Pentagrams

1.   Purpose - The pentagram is a symbol that represents the four elements and the spirit of divinity. Using this symbol helps communicate to our subconscious that the energies we are evoking are of the natural elements. Our subconscious knows what these elements are, we naturally respond to the change of seasons and to interaction of a given element. Using the pentagram we are telling our subconscious not only that we are working with these concepts at an energetic level, but also providing instruction on how to do so.

2.   How - Via drawing and visualizing the pentagram in blue flame, we are sealing a space in a given direction with the intention and purpose to work with an elemental or divine correspondence.

11. Sealing the Space

1.   Purpose - As you conduct the LBRP you seal the space you are in. This creates a blessed and

cleansed sanctuary at a spiritual level via your visualizations. Within this space you eventually call down more divine light either through the process of sealing yourself in the energy as part of the LBRP, conducting the final Qabalistic Cross step, or even electing to perform the Analysis of the Keyword at the end.

2. How - At each phase of the LBRP you are evoking new energy after sealing your own aura. You are directing and instructing the energy to at minimum, cleanse and protect the space you are in to perform other rituals. The final aspect of cleansing after balancing the elements is to surround yourself in divine light, and seal all of this intentional energy into your aura. Additionally performing the optional Analysis of the Keyword saturates the space in divine light even further. One or all of these things will always provide some sort of fundamental cleansing as a result.

12. Qabalistic Cross:

1. Purpose - Seals in our aura

2. How - Via calling on "the source" and visualizing you being enveloped in it. In further context it also connects "the source" to the Earth to synchronize "above" and "below" so may influence both. In this case that influence is to provide protection and seal your aura. This is vocalized by the prayer you vibrate as you conduct the ritual. In the final step of the LBRP this is worth expounding on further as you are

sealing in a cleansed aura balanced by the elements.

Custom Ritual

This ritual will be called the *Meditation of the Pentagram.* It is entirely informal, and created for the purpose of this text to show practitioners how to create their own rituals. The intent is that you will create a very small cleansed space in which you can meditate and focus on each element. This is also inspired by a concept you may wish to learn later known as Archangel Meditation. This takes the LBRP's fundamentals, and helps one focus solely on the product of the LBRP in a meditative state.

1. Begin by identifying the four cardinal directions in relation to where you are standing. Face *East.*
2. Perform the Qabalistic Cross.
3. As you conduct the next steps, draw each pentagram immediately beside you. This is so you can perform this in any size of space, not just a room where you must walk.
4. Now draw the banishing pentagram in the East like you normally would, but simply begin moving to face *South* once you have drawn it. No need to chant any mantras or visualize anything, other than being immersed in white light and seeing the pentagrams you draw.
5. Once again draw a banishing pentagram for the South, then face *West.*
6. Now draw the pentagram for the West and face *North.*

7.   Finally, draw the banishing pentagram while facing North, then return to facing *East*.

8.   Now that you are facing East again, feel free to stand, sit, or lie down in the center of the space you are in.

9.   Close your eyes, inhale, and see all the pentagrams flame brightly around you.

10. Begin performing the Four Fold Breath. You will do this four times total before focusing solely on meditation.

11. On the first iteration of the Four Fold Breath begin to visualize Raphael as a yellow light or an angel in yellow robes just like you would have in the LBRP.

12. On the next iteration visualize Michael on your right as a red light or angel in red robes.

13. On the third iteration visualize Gabriel behind you as a blue light or an angel in blue robes.

14. On the final iteration visualize Uriel on your left as a green light or an angel in green robes.

15. Now conduct the Four Fold Breath again, but don't stop after one iteration. Continue this for the remainder of the ritual until you are ready to conclude.

16. Inhale and visualize all the angels, pentagrams, and the white light around you glow even more vibrant.

17. As you hold your breath focus on the visualization. Be present, try to feel each elemental energy coming from the directions they correspond to.

18. Exhale and feel yourself rest in this energy, continue to feel it.

19. As you hold your breath focus on Raphael.

20. Repeat steps 16 through 19, but as you reach step 19 each time, switch to a different angel. Next would be Michael, followed by Gabriel, and lastly Uriel.

21. Continue to repeat these steps as many times as you like. Grow the energy and connect to it, strengthen your visualizations therein.

22. Once you are ready to conclude, gradually open your eyes. Perform the Qabalistic Cross again, then perform the Sign of Silence. This concludes the ritual.

Hopefully via this simple meditation you can see how we took the correspondences and concepts that we know work from the LBRP, and apply them to a completely different type of exercise. Here we aren't necessarily cleansing a space, but we are still cleansing our aura and focusing on balancing the elements. This type of meditation can help one gain a deeper introspective understanding of each angel and element by simply being present and spending time with each. In this way, one who does this meditation frequently will gradually begin to understand the purpose each element serves in their own life, and by proxy, allow them to be more in tune with the natural elements we all experience day to day.

Using this exact same break down of a formula for a ritual in magick, go and try to modify a ritual of your choosing. Once you have successfully modified a ritual, try creating a brand new one like this meditation. Modification should be a bit easier as you can determine right away whether the desired effect is taking place. Once you create a new ritual, you may have to experiment with some trial and error. Remember the more complex the reference formula and correspondences, the more complex your new ritual will be. This just leaves logical room for error. Using meditation at first is not necessary, but it can make things a bit easier as meditation doesn't require a specific out come, just a specific focus. That focus can be anything, so this can help you get more familiar with how you respond to certain correspondences before constructing a ritual that is more extrospective focused rather than introspectively focused.

Your Will

It has been emphasized several times in this text that you are aiming to identify and act on your true will. This is unique to every individual consciousness that exists. As you continue to practice Ceremonial Magick with this focus, eventually you will see it begin to unravel. As that will becomes more and more clear to you, you will begin to naturally think of information and ideas you have not thought of before. This is because you have shifted your active consciousness and your subconscious to be in line with the energy the universe is creating. This shift causes a profound change within us that allows us to begin living our true purpose, this is our true will.

As your will becomes clear, you will begin to conduct rituals that focus more and more on that will. This works to naturally uncover your true will further, until it is ultimately the clearest thing in your life. Once you begin fully living in line with your true will, the process of growing to achieve TGW will also begin to come naturally. You will be able to guide yourself using your knowledge and purpose to achieve the next step each and every time. At first you will still need to learn the various established methods and rituals to help you get to the next step in your practice, but eventually you will need none of these things.

The most daunting thing about this self guidance is being certain that what you are learning is truly representative of what you can experience. Discovering one's true will is fairly straightforward. You will know because you will be doing it, it will be easy to see. Even if natural anxiety comes to challenge that notion, you will be able to fight back with your natural actions. On the other hand, knowing one has achieved TGW is both confusing and extremely obvious.

The confusing part is that once you have achieved TGW, you will know. This notion implies you *will* know, but not *how* you will know. Many people have done this work, but the way we can tell from the outside is if they actually claim to have completed it to begin with. Obviously that claim is contextual, but one who has achieved TGW is a complete consciousness. They have no need to learn from others, and often rarely would even teach others. They are too focused on applying their will and being inline with "the source". Their actions will be that of divinity and completeness, free of want, need, or desire for anything. This is because they are complete. You'll know you have completed it because this is how you will experience the rest of your life for eternity. It should be incredibly obvious to you, but from the outside looking in no one may ever know. We can only know when one most certainly hasn't achieved TGW but is claiming to, not the other way around.

This is almost by design, it is even true in other practices that teach a concept of achieving some sort of enlightenment. This is because it is not about others or what they think, it is about you and your path. We each have to cross the abyss on our own. This journey is not about other individuals, it is about everything in the universe. With that, enjoy your path and embrace it. Worry not where others are at, and try to refrain yourself from comparing your pacing in your practice to others. They should almost never be same outside of fundamentals, and as such can't be compared accurately anyway.

More importantly be sure to remain vigilant in identifying practitioners and teachers that claim to have achieved a higher status. While some of these people could mean absolutely no harm, and be wonderful, this notion in itself is a good indicator that the individual may have lost focus on the purpose of their practice. With this in mind, do seek teachers, seek community, and seek balance wherever you need it as you continue your path, it is yours. Above all though, seek yourself, and grow.

Celebrate

Welcome fellow Magickian, it is time to celebrate! In fact it has actually been time to celebrate since the moment you completed your first energy work exercise. In Ceremonial Magick there aren't really holidays or special occasions. Some choose to follow magickally inspired religions like Norse Paganism, Wicca, and Thelema. These, and many others, contain various holidays that align with Ceremonial

Magick practices. Others may observe significant planetary movements outside of a religious practice to celebrate or perform rituals. Even if you have no interest in any of these add-ons to your path, Ceremonial Magick does have one tradition that is pure celebration. This is known as "Cakes and Ale". Cakes and Ale is also celebrated by Wiccan practices, and is essentially a form of communion that you can take after ritual work. It can be taken alone or with a group. It is a great excuse to reward yourself for your work, or throw a party to gather with loved ones.

Ceremonial Magickians often elect to partake in Cakes and Ale after achieving a milestone in their ritual work. For example, you could have celebrated Cakes and Ale after learning each ritual taught in this book. It is a way to acknowledge and reward all the hard work you did and acknowledge your growth. Partaking in Cakes and Ale is simple, and often very fun. You don't even need Cakes or Ale. The idea of cake is to represent something sweet, or just a treat of any flavor you like. For your celebration you should enjoy your favorite food or treat. Same with ale, this simply represents a drink you enjoy, it can be alcohol, juice, tea, or even water. As long as whatever you drink is your favorite, then incorporate that into your celebration. Below are some practices you may wish to observe when celebrating Cakes and Ale.

- ✦ Bless your "cake" and "ale" with the intention of reaching your next step on your path, or reinforce the energy from the achievement you are celebrating.
- ✦ Invite loved ones to celebrate with you and throw a party. It can be a small gathering or a full blown celebration, it is up to you!

✦ Perform a group ritual from what you learned if applicable.

✦ Reflect and give thanks for what you've learned and your growth.

Now that you know how to celebrate Cakes and Ale, I personally wish you many amazing celebrations as you go forward. Please go celebrate right away you have more than earned it! Remember, as above, so below. As within, so without

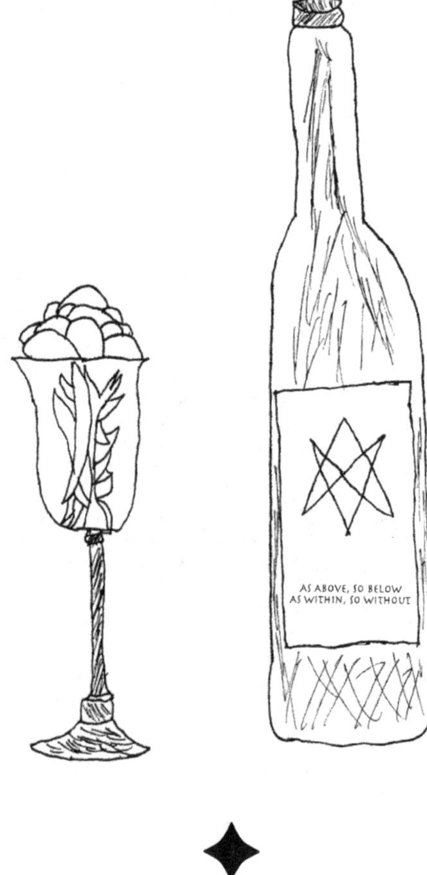

Works Cited

1. Barrett, Francis. "The Magus." The Magus, Book Ii: The Cabala; or The Secret Mysteries of Ceremonial Magic: Chapter Xiv: Of the Calculating Art of Such Names by the Tradition of Cabalists, Lackington, Alley, and Co., Temple of the Muses, 1801. Oct. 2002, https://www.sacred-texts.com/grim/magus/ma226.htm. Accessed 11 May 2022.

2. Britannica, The Editors of Encyclopedia. "energy". *Encyclopedia Britannica*, 16 November 2021, https://www.britannica.com/science/energy. Accessed 16 April 2022.

3. Britannica, The Editors of Encyclopedia. "zazen". *Encyclopedia Britannica*, 10 November 2016, https://www.britannica.com/topic/zazen.

4. Drake, Gordon W.F. "The First Law of Thermodynamics." *Encyclopedia Britannica*, Encyclopedia Britannica, Inc., 1 June 2021, https://www.britannica.com/science/thermodynamics/The-first-law-of-thermodynamics. Accessed 16 April 2022.

5. Drake, Gordon W.F. "The First Law of Thermodynamics." *Encyclopedia Britannica*, Encyclopedia Britannica, Inc., 1 June 2021, https://www.britannica.com/science/thermodynamics/The-second-law-of-thermodynamics. Accessed 16 April 2022.

6. Echols, Damien. "Angels and Archangels: A Magician's Guide." Sounds True, 2020.

7. Regardie, Israel. "How to Make and Use Talismans." New Falcon Publications, 2018.

8. "Occult 3." *Merriam-Webster.com Dictionary*, Merriam-Webster, https://www.merriam-webster.com/dictionary/occult. Accessed 17 April 2022.

9. Wikipedia Contributors. "Friction." Wikipedia, 12 April 2022, en.wikipedia.org/w/index.php?title=Friction&oldid=1082223658. Accessed 15 April 2022

10. Wikipedia Contributors. Pentagram. In Wikipedia. 12 April 2022, https://en.wikipedia.org/w/index.php?title=Pentagram. Accessed 17 April 2022.

11. Wikipedia Contributors. "Theban Alphabet." Wikipedia, 8 February 2022, en.wikipedia.org/w/index.php?title=Theban_alphabet&oldid=1070674685. Accessed 25 April 2022.

Bibliography

1. Avery, Maximus T. Book of the Hidden Name - Magick of the Shem HaMephorash Angels. Maximus Tyrannus Avery, 2020.
2. Brand, Damon, The 72 Angels of Magick: Instant Access to the Angels of Power (The Gallery of Magick). CreateSpace Independent Publishing Platform, 2016.
3. Echols, Damien. Angels & Archangels: A Magician's Guide. Sounds True, 2020.
4. Echols, Damien. High Magick: A Guide to the Spiritual Practices That Saved My Life on Death Row. Sounds True, 2018.
5. Louv, Jason. John Dee and the Empire of Angels Enochian Magick and the Occult Roots of the Modern World. Inner Traditions, 2018.
6. McHenry, Travis. Angel Tarot. Rockpool Publishing, 2020.

Index

About the Author

Casey Erdmann is a Ceremonial Magickian that has spent years practicing this craft. Through the years Casey became ordained, and began incorporating elements of the Thelema religion into his Ceremonial Magick practice. While diving deeper into his spirituality, Casey has simultaneously maintained an extremely active career in computer and information security for almost a decade. He has worn the hats of a software developer, a manager, a security analyst, and for the last 4 years, a hacker. Casey has a broad range of both philosophical and technical skills between these two passions, and uses them in tandem wherever possible.

In addition to his career work, currently Casey continues to both teach and practice Ceremonial Magick, as well as offensive security to individuals, universities, and private organizations alike. On a more personal note, Casey is a musician with several active music projects, and is a podcast host for the Echo's Box podcast. He is the proud care taker of Echo and Luna, his two dogs, and enjoys a good glass of bourbon (good to know if you need to grab his attention). To learn more visit https://echosbox.com and follow @echos.box and @itsjonesmusic on Instagram.